AF575535

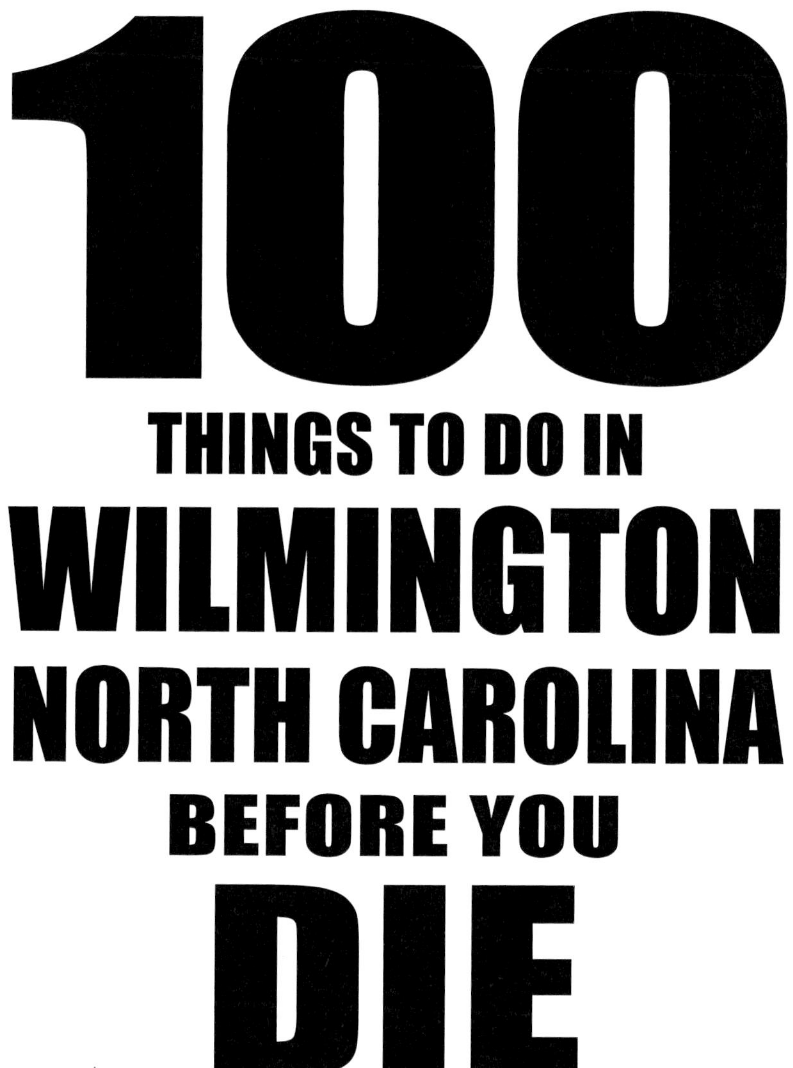
100
THINGS TO DO IN
WILMINGTON
NORTH CAROLINA
BEFORE YOU
DIE

Courtesy of New Hanover County

100 THINGS TO DO IN WILMINGTON NORTH CAROLINA BEFORE YOU DIE

AMY CONRY DAVIS

Reedy Press
PO Box 5131
St. Louis, MO 63139, USA
www.reedypress.com

Library of Congress Control Number: 2023951765

ISBN: 9781681065236

Design by Jill Halpin

Cover image courtesy of New Hanover County

Printed in the United States of America
24 25 26 27 28   5 4 3 2 1

DEDICATION

To Roy

Enjoy Wilmington!

Courtesy of Mayfaire

CONTENTS

Music and Entertainment

Sports and Recreation

Culture and History

ACKNOWLEDGMENTS

To Ben, who makes the ordinary adventurous. To Dad, who made the faraway possible, and Mom, who taught me to find fun in the close-to-home. To the family and friends who gave support, enthusiasm, and encouragement. To the kind folks at Reedy Press who put this opportunity in front of me and guided me through the process. To Connie Nelson of the Wilmington and Beaches Convention and Visitors Bureau, the City of Wilmington, New Hanover County, and others for their valuable assistance and input. Lastly, to Wilmington, its people, and its places.

PREFACE

I came to know Wilmington by way of Jacksonville, North Carolina, which is 45 minutes up the road. My family was stationed at Marine Corps Base Camp Lejeune, and the drive down Highway 17 was one we did often. I moved to the Port City as a single woman in my 20s, on the hunt for my first apartment and "grown-up" job. Twenty-odd years later, having moved away more than once, I live here with a husband and son and work as a freelancer. Wilmington has become my unofficial hometown.

I'm no expert on Wilmington, but live somewhere long enough and you eventually come to know it like the back of your hand. I could tell you all about the prettiest roads to drive, the most beautiful trees, the best shortcuts and back ways, and so on. I've also seen buildings razed and beloved businesses close and a population boom bring vision, development, and traffic. The highlight of working on this guidebook was the chance to merge past with present, to reconcile fond memories with an exciting wave of change.

In doing so, it was no easy task to pare down my choices for these entries. A geographic location can't be so easily distilled into any singular point of view. These are just the personal favorites of a semi-local crafted from experiences and time spent as a Wilmingtonian. To newcomers, I hope this book helps you choose your own adventures. To those who feel you've seen and

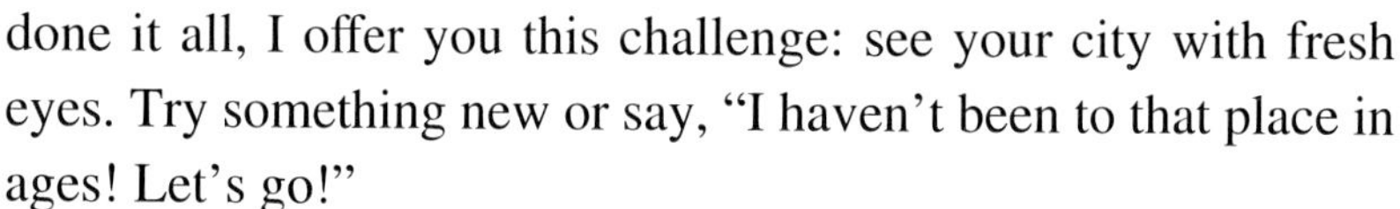

done it all, I offer you this challenge: see your city with fresh eyes. Try something new or say, “I haven’t been to that place in ages! Let’s go!”

Courtesy of Mayfaire

FOOD AND DRINK

INDULGE YOUR SWEET TOOTH AT BRITT'S DONUTS

The mere mention of the name "Britt's" is enough to elicit childlike glee in its fans. To understand the reason behind the unbridled enthusiasm, visit (March through September) this family-owned shop on the Carolina Beach Boardwalk and see the smiles for yourself. They've been cranking out warm, sugary doughnuts for nearly 90 years in a space that's basically standing room only. Don't bother asking for a menu though—they only make a glaze flavor—and the beverage choices are only coffee, milk, or fountain drinks. Rain or shine, there'll be a long line out the door, so come prepared to wait. And to save yourself the misery of losing your spot, it's important to mention: leave the plastic at home. Britt's is an old-school, cash-only enterprise.

Carolina Beach Boardwalk
910-707-0755
brittsdonutshop.com

TIP

The town of Carolina Beach has dozens of free summer activities from outdoor movies at the lake, family nights at the gazebo, to weekly fireworks at the Boardwalk.

2

NOSH
ON A TROLLY STOP DOG

The humble hot dog doesn't always get the recognition it deserves. But when you come across one done right, it hits the spot. Starting at about $3 a dog, Trolly Stop's reasonable prices mean you can feed your whole crew and sample more than one of their signature weenies with all the "fixins." Bite into the North Carolina (mustard, chili, and slaw) or the Battleship (mustard, salsa, onions, and tomatoes) or create your own masterpiece. Their list of toppings includes sliced cukes, kraut, bacon bits, and a famous secret hot sauce that gives you plenty to work with. In addition to all-beef and pork sausages, Trolly Stop's menu has soy-based and fat-free turkey dogs, too. Hit the Lumina Avenue shop after a day at the beach or visit Fountain Drive by UNCW.

94 S Lumina Ave., Wrightsville Beach, 910-256-3421
4502 Fountain Dr., 910-452-3952
trollystophotdogs.com

3

SHUCK A PAIL
ON THE OYSTER TRAIL

Fresh, local seafood is easy to come by in this region, but we're particularly proud of our oysters. The shallow, salty marshes along our coastline and moderate temperatures of our waters make an ideal combination for thriving oyster habitats. Wild oyster populations have dwindled over the years, but a revival in the industry has contributed to reef restoration and protection, as well as an increase in cultivated varieties. Aquaculture production is on the rise and many of the area's oyster farmers offer tours and tastings. You can also find their harvests on the menus of nearby restaurants. From wild Stump Sound oysters to farm-raised Stones Bay and Tarheel Tiderunners—raw, steamed, or fried—there's no wrong way to enjoy a briny bivalve.

ncoystertrail.org

TIP

For the squeamish or skeptical, an oyster roast is an excellent introduction to *Ostreidae*. Light the grill; throw on a bushel; and add sausage, potatoes, and corn on the cob into the mix.

A FEW RESTAURANTS SERVING LOCAL OYSTERS AND SEAFOOD

Catch Restaurant
6623 Market St., 910-799-3847
catchwilmington.com

PinPoint Restaurant
114 Market St., 910-769-2972
pinpointrestaurant.com

Ceviche's
7210 Wrightsville Ave., 910-256-3131
wbceviche.com

Seabird
1 S Front St., 910-769-5996
seabirdnc.com

4

BITE
INTO WILMINGTON'S BEST BURGERS

Ever since "Hamburger Charlie" stole the show at the 1885 Erie County Fair, our nation has been slightly obsessed with patties on buns. Wilmington shares in this fervor, and the following list is proof. Winnie's Tavern has been honking the "best burger" horn for decades. The decor and menu have evolved since its early days, but the Classic still hits where it counts. You'll always find P.T.'s hopping at lunch or dinner. Mark your preferences on the order sheet and grab a hand-squeezed lemonade while you wait for your meal. The Fork N Cork doesn't call its burgers Hot Mess and Hay Dios Mio for nothing, so bring your A-game. And downtown's Copper Penny, beloved for its people-pleasing pub food, makes a mean cheeseburger with a kids' version, too.

TIP

Port City Taste, which lasts 14 days, is an excellent way to discover all manner of delicious local menus, including more burgers!

Winnie's Tavern
1895 Burnett Blvd., 910-762-1799
wilmingtonsbestburger.com

P.T.'s Olde Fashioned Grille
4544 Fountain Dr., 910-392-2293
8116 Market St., 910-686-6550
1437 Military Cutoff Rd., 910-256-8850
ptsgrille.com

Fork N Cork
122 Market St., 910-228-5247
theforkncork.com

Copper Penny
109 Chestnut St., 910-762-1373
copperpennync.com

5

HAVE
A HEARTY DINER BREAKFAST

The South knows a thing or two about the most important meal of the day, and a "greasy spoon" is your best bet for unpretentious comfort food. These diners are nothing fancy, but the grub is stick-to-your-ribs satisfying and the coffee refills unlimited. Dixie Grill goes all out with Belgian waffles, pancakes, and French toast. Jimbo's is up with the sun through to the lunch hour, so you get to decide if it's a quiche or rib-eye steak kind of day. For 50 years, Salt Works has kept a good thing going and could last five more decades with its grits and home fries alone. Goody Goody is known for its Spanish omelets, served any way you ask. Try one with fruit and cheese or Mexican chili for a unique twist.

Dixie Grill
116 Market St., 910-762-7280
dixiegrillwilmington.com

Jimbo's Breakfast & Lunch House
1529 S College Rd., 910-799-2211
jimbosbreakfastandlunch.com

The Original Salt Works
6301 Oleander Dr., 910-350-0018
@theoriginalsaltworks

Goody Goody Omelet House
3817 Market St., 910-762-0444
goodygoodyhouse.com

6

SHARE A FEAST FROM THE FAR EAST

AT INDOCHINE

Once you step inside Indochine, you'll understand what the fuss is all about. Every nook and cranny of this restaurant is beautifully adorned with murals, Buddha statues, and Asian art. In the back, the outdoor dining garden is an oasis of trees and tiki huts. And the Thai-Vietnamese cuisine delivers the savory kick you came in for. The menu might intimidate first-timers but the curries (Massaman comes highly recommended) are a good start. To dial up (or back) on the heat, the dishes can be made to order with little to no spice up to five-alarm Thai hot. Wash it down with a Naga Knockout from the bar and save room for the mango and sticky rice dessert.

7 Wayne Dr., 910-251-9229
indochinewilmington.com

7

DRINK LOCAL "JOE"

That first cup of coffee matters, and the shop you buy it from should, too. Whether you're in need of a quick drive-through or somewhere to sit awhile, make a point to pick a locally owned establishment for your caffeine fix. Community-oriented Folks and Bitty & Beau's will have you feeling downright neighborly no matter how long you stay. The Port City Java chain is proudly born and brewed in our fair city and a daily routine for a lot of Wilmingtonians. Casa Blanca's decor channels sunny, minimalist vibes. And SUNdays, on the second floor of the South End Surf Shop at Wrightsville Beach, gives you lattes and London Fog with views of the Atlantic.

Folks Café
1201 Princess St., 910-362-1448
facebook.com/folksilm

Bitty & Beau's Coffee
4949 New Centre Dr. (flagship location), 910-769-1252
bittyandbeauscoffee.com

Port City Java
21A N Front St. (flagship location), 910-762-5282
portcityjava.com

Casa Blanca Coffee Roasters
7409 Market St., 910-821-0639
casablancacoffee.co

SUNdays
708B S Lumina Ave., Wrightsville Beach, 910-256-2011
facebook.com/sundayswb

8

TRAVEL
WITHOUT A PASSPORT

Tap into Wilmington's international community and transport yourself to a different country each night of the week. For a small town, our food scene is surprisingly diverse and the chefs at these restaurants are skillfully adept at remastering traditional recipes. Have a seat at Savorez for Latin-inspired arepas and empanadas with a coastal touch or the German Cafe for schnitzel and bier. On Oleander Drive, Olympia has been wowing customers with its Greek spanakopita since 1994. Family-owned La Costa has three locations for caldo de mariscos, and some of the best Indian lassi and lamb vindaloo comes from Tandoori Bites. When France calls to you, be sure to answer back and dive into a plate of steak frites at Brasserie du Soleil.

TIP

Continue the quest for global inspiration at UNCW's InterCultural Festival, the Wilmington Greek Festival, or St. Stan's Polish Festival in Castle Hayne.

Savorez Restaurant
402 Chestnut St., 910-833-8894
savorez.com

The German Cafe
316 Nutt St., 910-763-5523
thegermancafe.com

Olympia
5629 Oleander Dr., 910-796-9636
olympiawilmington.com

La Costa Mexican Restaurant
3617 Market St. (flagship location), 910-772-9000
lacostanc.com

Tandoori Bites
1620 S College Rd., 910-794-4545
tandooribites.net

Brasserie du Soleil
1908 Eastwood Rd., 910-256-2226
brasseriedusoleil.com

9

FOLLOW
THE ALE TRAIL

In a few short years, a frenzied explosion of beer-happy businesses has put enough dots on the map to warrant the need for a full-fledged guide. You can easily strike out on your own, but to blaze this boozy trail right, try out a digital passport. Download the mobile pass (day and annual options available) from the Wilmington Ale Trail's website and you'll have all the info you need in the palm of your hand. You'll get news on the latest happenings, vouchers, and all the pertinent info for navigating the beer scene. There's also a free print magazine listing these bottleshops, breweries, and bars. On your travels, pay homage to the OG that started it all, Front Street Brewery, with a flight of flagship beers.

wilmingtonaletrail.com

TIP

For a safe, hassle-free experience, book with Port City Brew Bus or Roadies Local. For slightly more adventure, take in one of the pedal-powered options like Trolley Pub or BrewBoat.

10

HIT THE ROOF(TOPS)

When you're perched above the city with a bird's-eye view, somehow the drinks taste better. Catch a well-timed sunset or wait until the stars come out for an "elevated" experience at one of our rooftop bars. Either way, unobstructed views will be on full display. At the historic Coastline Center, guests and outside visitors can gather at Marriott's trendy bistro, aView. The menu lists shareable plates, desserts, and wines by the glass or bottle. Over at Cloud 9, part of Embassy Suites, cleverly named cocktails like Bullet with Butterfly Wings, Tonight Tonight, and Neon Angels await you. Take in the trifecta of DJs, drinks, and dancing upstairs at the Rooftop Bar, and for more live music and daily entertainment, work your way up three floors to the Reel Cafe.

aView Rooftop Bar and Bistro (at Aloft Wilmington Coastline Center)
501 Nutt St., 910-377-7600
marriott.com

Cloud 9 Rooftop Bar (Embassy Suites)
9 Estell Lee Pl., 910-726-9227
cloud9ilm.com

The Rooftop Bar (North Front Theatre)
21 N Front St., 910-833-5886
rooftopbarwilmington.com

The Reel Cafe
100 S Front St., 910-251-1832
reelcafe.net

11

SCARF DOWN CHIPS AND SALSA

AT K38

Once the first basket of chips and salsa hits your table at K38, you'll be hooked. This pairing is a perfect combination of salt, spice, and crunch. And they'll happily provide refills until you're fit to burst. While you nibble, soak in the Baja-inspired decor and surf videos playing on the big-screen TVs. Feel free to order a Blue Agave margarita to complete the daydream. The Wannabe, Pomerita, or Pineapple Jalapeño flavors (frozen, blended, or on the rocks) are where it's at. It'll be hard but try to save room for your meal—everything from the roadside tacos to mahi wraps and shrimp tempura rolls are tasty. For poco mas, tack on a side order of black beans, Mexican rice, or cheesy potato cakes.

5410 Oleander Dr., 910-395-6040
8211 Market St., 910-686-8211
1127 Military Cutoff Rd., 910-679-4009
3846 Carolina Beach Rd., 910-500-6844
k38bajagrill.com

Tower 7 Baja Mexican Grill: 4 N Lumina Ave., Wrightsville Beach
910-256-8585, tower7.com

TIP

To stock up on homemade salsa and chips, stop at kBueno Cocina. It's next door to the Oleander Drive restaurant and open Monday through Sunday.

12

PICK YOUR OWN FRUIT

AT LEWIS NURSERY AND FARMS

For three generations, Lewis Nursery and Farms has been in the business of growing strawberries, blueberries, raspberries, and blackberries. Come berry-picking season, people show up en masse eager to pluck the ripe, juicy bounty from the fields of this family farm. A nibble or two of the wares is part of the fun. The process is simple: grab a bucket, work your way through the plants, and then take your haul to be weighed and priced. You also have the option of ditching all the work completely to grab a rocking chair and snack on homemade ice cream. Retail spaces, available at both locations, sell a variety of take-home, ready-made products. During offseason, their holiday buckets overflow with jams, jellies, and cookies and have all the makings for a perfect gift.

6517 Gordon Rd.
2746 Swartville Rd., Castle Hayne, 910-452-9659
lewisfarms.com

TIP

For more berries, bands, and beer, check out the North Carolina Blueberry Festival in Burgaw.

13

EAT YOUR VEGETABLES

For those whose palates prefer garden greens, plant-based dining options are aplenty. Black Sea Grill puts out Mediterranean-inspired salads, kebabs, and appetizers for lunch and dinner. The Vegetarian Combo with hummus, falafel, eggplant, and stuffed grape leaves provides the whole array. Sealevel Diner is 100 percent vegan to its tempeh and tofu core while Blue Surf throws Wild Mushroom Pizza Bread and Hippy Breakfast into the mix. Build your own bowls at Epic Food and make sure the roasted chickpeas are part of your order. At the Green House Restaurant, the eco-friendly experience extends beyond the entrées to include the building materials, composting, and water conservation.

TIP

Community Supported Agriculture (CSA) pairs consumers with local growers. Feast Down East and the NC Cooperative Extension are two helpful resources for information on participating farms.

Black Sea Grill
118 S Front St., 910-254-9990
blackseagrill.com

Sealevel City Vegan Diner
1015 S Kerr Ave., 910-833-7196
@sealevelcitydiner

Blue Surf Cafe
250 Racine Dr. (flagship location), 910-523-5362
bluesurfrestaurants.com

Epic Food Co.
1113 Military Cutoff Rd., 910-679-4216
epicfoodonline.com

The Green House Restaurant
1427 Military Cutoff Rd., 910-679-4994
thegreenrestaurant.com

SPLURGE ON A SECOND SCOOP

AT BOOMBALATTI'S

I scream. You scream. We all scream for Boombalatti's! The name is memorable and catchy and so are their dozens of homemade flavors. They've set up shop in three locations now, so you'll find them in the Forum, Hampstead, and NoFo district downtown. However you roll—cone, cup, or dish—every scoop is made with milk from happy, grass-fed cows. Work your way through the list, sampling Birthday Cake, Banana Pudding, or Black Sesame Brittle until you find what speaks to your taste buds. To fill your own freezer, get a Boom-Box delivered to your doorstep, loaded with your favorite pints. And how fun is this? You can book Boombalatti's VW Bus, Sprinkles, to show up at your next party with frozen desserts to share with your guests.

127 Military Cutoff Rd., 910-679-4955
1005 N 4th St., 910-660-8244
15919 Hwy. 17 N, 910-821-1140
boombalattis.com

15

TAKE HOME A TREAT
FROM APPLE ANNIE'S

For any occasion that requires baked goods (don't they all?), save yourself the drive and head to Apple Annie's first. Pies, cheesecakes, breads, cookies—if it's made with flour and butter, you'll find it in one of their cases. The bakers here could whip up these recipes in their sleep; they're so good at it. The original bakery got its start in New Jersey but moved down south to Wilmington about 30 years ago. Since then, the shop has grown and expanded but the quality hasn't wavered. Whether it's an apple Danish for one or lemon chiffon cakes for a room of 20, they can accommodate orders of all sizes. As an added bonus, many of their products can be shipped nationwide.

837 S Kerr Ave., 910-799-9023
1121 Military Cutoff Rd., 910-256-6585
appleanniesbakeshop.com

16

GO BIG OR GO HOME
AT FLAMING AMY'S

Hot, fast, cheap, and easy. That's the slogan at Flaming Amy's Burrito Barn and it says it all. You might want to add H-U-G-E to the list, too. Their famous burritos have some heft to 'em (and they'll even "doublewide" your order by request) so wear your stretchy pants. A few winners are Nacho Daddy, Thai Mee Up, Tree Hugger, and Double Bypass, but nothing says you can't go with nachos, tacos, or quesadillas instead. Sweet tea refills are unlimited (just sayin') but they also have a full selection of craft beers to pick from. If you like your dishes with a dollop of heat, try one of everything at the homemade salsa bar.

4002 Oleander Dr., 910-799-2919
1140 N Lake Park Blvd., Carolina Beach, 910-458-2563
flamingamysburritobarn.com

TIP

Show off your ink on Taco and Tattoo Tuesdays to get a 10 percent discount.

17

DEVOUR AFTER HOURS
AT SLICE OF LIFE

Picture this: a cozy pizza joint, a table of friends sharing laughs, and a big pie with a pitcher of beer. Well, Slice of Life is like that. It's a solid, reliable place for consistently good pizza, and with four locations, there's one in your neck of the woods. They stay open until 3 a.m., so date night, late night, game night, family night, it's the place that works for anything. The chicken wings are top-notch, too, and go down easy with any of the beers they've got on tap. You might be surprised to learn they also have the biggest tequila selection in town, so flip a coin and find out who's gonna buy the first round.

125 Market St., 910-251-9444
1437 Military Cutoff Rd., Ste. 101, 910-256-2229
3715 Patriot Way, Unit 101, 910-799-1399
155 Porters Neck Rd., 910-686-3882
grabslice.com

18

SHOP THE STANDS
AT A FARMERS MARKET

It used to be that downtown's Riverfront market was the biggest farmers market in town. But, as demand has grown, a variety of weekly markets have begun taking hold in different neighborhoods. Buying your groceries at one of these markets gets you outdoors, connects you to the community, lets you make friends with farmers, and most importantly, lets you buy food that was grown a few miles down the road. They can be an excellent source for produce, meat, eggs, honey, baked goods, and even handmadc arts and crafts. Biggers has two locations now, and Carolina, Kure, and Wrightsville Beaches all have their own events. The one in Scotts Hill sets up every Wednesday on the front lawn of the Poplar Grove plantation. Each operates on its own schedule so check before you start out.

Riverfront Farmers Market
riverfrontfarmersmarket.org

Biggers Market
facebook.com/biggersmarket

Wrightsville Beach Farmers Market
townofwrightsvillebeach.com

Poplar Grove Farmers Market
facebook.com/farmersmarketpoplargrove

DISCOVER
A FAVORITE FOOD TRUCK

Mobile eats have gained traction here, and even some brick-and-mortar restaurants are opting to take their meals on wheels, so to speak. New businesses continue to pop up every day, but a handful of well-established, tried-and-true trucks have garnered quite the devout following. Breweries are your best bet for finding them parked, but most any festival or fair is sure to have a lineup. For the best in 'cue, Webo's, Poor Piggy's, and Rude Bwoys Jerk BBQ continue to rise above the rest. Get your fill of Maine's most popular crustacean at Lobster Dogs, or find dishes with an Asian flair at Bahn Sai. WilmyWoodie and Wheelz Pizza do hot pies, the First Bite shows up with breakfast, and Lane's Ferry grills cheesesteaks and hot dogs.

portcitydaily.com
nhcparksconservancy.org/food-truck-frolic

TIP

To follow these trucks and others, check out the Food Truck Tracker on Port City Daily's website. Also, a Food Truck Rodeo is hosted by the New Hanover County Parks Conservancy once a year.

20

FONDUE IT
AT LITTLE DIPPER

Fondue. You either love it or you love it. Who can resist dunking and dipping and all that hot, gooey cheese? At Little Dipper Fondue, nothing on the menu is one-size-fits-all so you're in full control of what's at the end of your long, pointy fork. Choose from a dozen different, drizzling sauces or broths as you work up from appetizers to the Full Fondue Experience. There are also dessert options for those who'd rather skip ahead to strawberries and melted chocolate. During holiday months, the menu takes on a seasonal touch with specialties such as peppermint eggnog, white chocolate, or winter gorgonzola cheese. When warmer weather hits, ask for a table on the back deck where you can enjoy your shared meal alfresco.

138 S Front St., 910-251-0433
littledipperfondue.com

21

BREAK BREAD
WITH NORTHSIDE FOOD CO-OP

The kind and concerned citizens behind the Northside Food Co-op have centered their mission on "ensuring food security" and "generating resilience" through education, empowerment, and access to healthy, affordable food. With the help of partners and sponsors, they host various programs, run Frankie's Outdoor Market, oversee a community garden, and manage an informative newsletter. They're also at work to bring a community-owned grocery store to the Northside neighborhood. What's more, they've put their message into action by hosting community dinners. In collaboration with volunteers, nonprofits, and local businesses, these monthly gatherings are meant to foster connection between all neighbors. Simple, nutritious meals are served as well as a come-as-you-are spirit of generosity. The events are free and open to anyone and everyone, from all parts of town.

northsidefoodcoop.com

DINE AT A STUDENT-RUN RESTAURANT AT CFCC

Booking a reservation at Our Place Restaurant requires a little extra legwork but it's a worthy cause, and for some people, one they come back to time and time again. It's part of the Cape Fear Community College Culinary Arts program and gives students real-world experience with both kitchen and front-of-house duties. The space looks and feels like any "real" working restaurant and holds up to 45 diners at a time. Meals are served once a week (every Wednesday) and they alternate lunch and dinner between spring and fall semesters. For $12 (dinner costs a few bucks more), you get a beverage, appetizer, entrée, and dessert. The chefs experiment with cuisines from around the globe, giving you a chance to choose from German, Greek, African, Asian, and more.

403 S Water St., Building W, 910-362-7143
cfcc.edu/our-place

TIP

Some other CFCC programs open to the public include haircuts, dental exams, and childcare services.

23

REQUEST A BALCONY SEAT
AT FLORIANA

Many will remember this one as the former location of Roy's Riverboat Landing, a restaurant that operated for nearly 40 years. In 2018, Floriana moved in and revamped everything from floor to ceiling, giving the place a completely refreshed makeover. What did remain, however, were the nine, private balconies on the second floor. With just enough room for a table for two, these cozy patios give you and your date an outstanding overlook from which to contemplate the street scenes down below. You'll have eyes on busy Water and Front Streets, the USS *North Carolina* across the river, and plenty of people-watching. Soak in your surroundings, using all your senses, as you enjoy a hearty plate of branzino or fettuccini Bolognese.

2 Market St., 910-504-0160
wilmington.florianarestaurant.com

Courtesy of the North Carolina Azalea Festival

MUSIC AND ENTERTAINMENT

24

HAVE A NIGHT OUT
AT THE WILSON CENTER

If dinner and a show have been on your mind for a while, this sleek performing arts center is the perfect candidate. The venue is within walking distance from dozens of downtown bars and restaurants so get gussied up, grab an Uber, and you're all set for an evening of entertainment. The Wilson Center at CFCC can accommodate more than 1,500 guests, and wheelchair-accessible seats, sign language, captioning, and large-print programs open the world of theater to all. Their programming covers Broadway plays, classical music concerts, dance, comedy, educational programs, and free community events. If you're feeling exceptionally fancy, go for the VIP treatment with the Opera Box Experience. The ticket comes with a number of perks including drinks, snacks, and appetizers from Ruth's Chris Steakhouse.

703 N 3rd St., 910-362-7913
wilsoncentertickets.com

25

TAKE A SEAT
FOR CINEMATIQUE

Historic Thalian Hall has been entertaining theatergoers since the mid-1800s. In fact, it's one of the only theaters in the United States still known to have the Thunder Roll, a special effect using cannon balls and wooden troughs. Operas, minstrel shows, pantomimes, military bands, even animals have made their debut on her main stage. Today, in addition to an all-encompassing performing arts calendar, it's been hosting a successful film series for nearly 30 years. Cinematique shows movies Monday through Wednesday with a focus on foreign and independent art-house films. Screenings are often held in the smaller Stein Theatre, but if you're lucky enough to catch one in the grand auditorium, you'll be blown away by the elaborate architectural details.

310 Chestnut St., 910-632-2285
thalianhall.org

LISTEN TO BLUES
AT THE RUSTY NAIL

Not everyone's familiar with the Nail, but it's a "hidden secret" worth venturing out for. For music lovers and fans of the blues, in particular, it's an institution. Part juke joint, part dive bar, it's just the sort of place that works for the soulful, somber sounds of the genre. Once a week, the Cape Fear Blues Society holds an open jam, which attracts both amateur and professional musicians from all over the region. You never know what the night will bring, but expect an eclectic mix of vocals, piano, guitars, and drums. In June, the sessions expand into a full two weeks of steady entertainment as the Cape Fear Blues Festival takes over. Many of the shows are free or a few bucks at the door.

1310 S 5th Ave., 910-251-1888

27

CATCH CUCALORUS FEVER
AT JENGO'S PLAYHOUSE

A dozen filmmakers calling themselves "Twinkle Doon" had a big idea to bring cinematic joy to the masses. That seed grew into the Cucalorus Film Festival, and now it's the biggest, weirdest, funkiest gathering of cinephiles to hit the Port City. Every November, the weeklong schedule overflows with parties, presentations, screenings, and installations. The venues are spread across town, but the festival's headquarters, Jengo's Playhouse, is where most of the magic happens. Hang around the place long enough, especially in the wee hours of the morning, and you're bound to be drawn into inevitable shenanigans. The Cucalorus crew brings the very best of documentaries, short films, features, and animation to their audiences. Most refreshingly, no prizes or awards are handed out, just claps and cheers for the craft.

815 Princess St., 910-343-5995
cucalorus.org

TIP

Jengo's can be found in the Soda Pop District, named so for the former Coca-Cola bottling plant. The neighborhood has been redeveloped in recent years and is now a haven for hip eateries and craft beer.

28

PARTY
AT A BEACH BAR

If there's one thing this town does really well, it's the beach bar. The atmosphere is relaxed, the drinks are cold, and everyone's on "island time" once they pass through the doors. Come straight from the water, flip-flops and all—there's no need to dress up unless you want to. From Kure Beach to Wrightsville, a few places stand out for their nightly entertainment and laid-back vibes. Catch a tiki show at Ocean Grill's pier or sip a frosty lager at the much-loved, definitely divey Fat Pelican. Dockside's view of the Intracoastal Waterway accompanied by a spicy Bloody Mary in hand should keep you entertained for hours. Lagerheads's front patio is made for people-watching, day or night, and the Palm Room's got live music.

Ocean Grill and Tiki Bar
1211 S Lake Park Blvd., 910-707-0049
oceangrilltiki.com

The Fat Pelican
8 S Lake Park Blvd., 910-458-4061
thefatpelican.com

Dockside Restaurant
1308 Airlie Rd., 910-256-2752
thedockside.com

Lagerheads Tavern
35 N Lumina Ave., Wrightsville Beach, 910-256-0171

The Palm Room
11 E Salisbury St., Wrightsville Beach, 910-509-3040

ATTEND
THE NORTH CAROLINA AZALEA FESTIVAL

Every spring, our gardens and parks explode into a riot of color. Azaleas bloom in pinks, reds, whites, and coral, and we go crazy for it. These classy rhododendrons are so special, in fact, that we throw a big bash for them every year. The North Carolina Azalea Festival, which began in 1948, is a massive, community-wide celebration with garden parties, home tours, street fair, parade, and live music. It's estimated that some 300,000 attendees take part in the five-day event, and notable past visitors have included Michael Jordan, Ronald Reagan, Andy Griffith, and Kelly Ripa. The Festival Queen and Princess nominations are a main attraction, especially the coronation ceremony. Its culmination is marked by a spectacular fireworks display, which takes place over the Cape Fear River.

ncazaleafestival.org

TIP

The entire town gets in the mood with festival-inspired menus, cocktails, and events. Over in the Brooklyn Arts District, the Alt-Zalea Festival spotlights an array of live local music.

30

CLAP FOR CLASS ACTS
AT KENAN AUDITORIUM

One of the biggest perks of a college town is having access to the robust cultural arts program on campus. UNCW's Kenan Auditorium, managed by the Office of the Arts, is a 1,000-seat venue with a nonstop lineup of local, national, and internationally acclaimed artists. On any given day, you'll find headlining acts, comedians, dancers, films, and performances—not to mention the talents of the Music and Theatre Departments, Wilmington Symphony Orchestra, Opera Wilmington, Chamber Music Wilmington, and North Carolina Youth Tap Ensemble. Tickets can be purchased online or by calling the box office. No permit or pass is required for parking during an event, and the building is conveniently located near the Randall Drive entrance off College Road.

515 Wagoner Dr., 910-962-3500
uncw.edu/arts/kenan

31

PLAY POOL
AT BLUE POST

Grown-ups, 21 and over, are welcome to let their inner child out to play at this easygoing bar. Blue Post Billiards is all about fun and games, and they make it easy with rooms of billiards, air hockey, Skee-Ball, arcade games, and darts. For even more healthy competition, players can hit up Free Pool Mondays for extra practice on their bank shot. They don't serve food, but the straightforward drink menu has beer and liquor as well as daily specials. You will need to buy a one-time membership (don't worry, it's only a buck), but that's where the hard work ends. Once inside, find a comfy couch, bask in the glow of string lights and neon, and sip PBR late into the night.

15 S Water St., 910-343-1141
facebook.com/bluepostbilliards

32

GET WEIRD
AT THE MUSEUM OF THE BIZARRE

Quirky, peculiar, offbeat. If your ears perked up at that, then get in line for this tourist attraction. At $3 a ticket, you won't break the bank no matter how many times you have to come back to settle the debate over whether the chupacabra's hand is real or not. The Museum of the Bizarre also has an eerie mirror maze and enough scary dolls and doodads to last a lifetime. The young, the curious, and the macabre will undoubtedly be grossed out or entertained. It's located in the center of the action on Water Street so you can easily bookend your visit with a Riverwalk stroll and a meal. Pop in for an afternoon, suspend your disbelief, and let the strange and supernatural rule for a bit.

201 S Water St., 910-399-2641
museumbizarre.com

33

HANG WITH THE COOL KIDS

AT SATELLITE BAR AND LOUNGE

The next time you're trying to decide where to meet up with friends, go where the cool kids hang out. Satellite's bartenders are well-versed in craft beer, and the bar carries more brands than you can shake a stick at. Between movie nights, karaoke, Latin dance, and all manner of live music, this funky joint is always buzzing. Sunday nights are no different. Their bluegrass jam is a talented group of local musicians who gather to play spirited renditions of mountain tunes. They've been pickin' and strummin' here for many moons and know how to bring the energy. Barstool or bench? It won't matter. You'll be on your feet in no time.

120 Greenfield St., 910-399-2796
facebook.com/satellitebarandlounge

TIP

Don’t forget about Block Taco around the corner. When you see the (fake) donkey, on top of the car, wearing a sombrero—you’re in the right place.

LAUGH IT UP
AT DEAD CROW COMEDY ROOM

This comedy club got its start in a basement, but now comedians of all genres have a fresh scene on Third Street to test out new material. Dead Crow's lineup of entertainment is a mix of comedic acts with a sprinkling of improv and open mic nights. From sweating, nervous newcomers to smooth, stand-up legends, you'll see it all. Slapstick, satire, self-deprecating humor—whatever makes you chuckle, you'll find it here, and the intimate setting undoubtedly makes the joke and punchlines even . . . punchier. Food trucks drop in on a rotating schedule, and the neighboring business, Lush Garden Bar, has got what you need for drinks. Loud LOLs are appreciated, of course, but swallow any undue outbursts by sipping on a Heckler cocktail instead.

511 N 3rd St., 910-399-1750
deadcrowcomedy.com

TIP

Hone your stand-up skills and ask the folks at DCCR about local comedians who teach improv or comedy-writing classes.

35

MAKE A BEELINE
FOR THE BROOKLYN ARTS DISTRICT

The multimillion-dollar restoration of St. Andrew's Church (now Brooklyn Arts Center) in the early 2000s brought a newfound creative energy to this neighborhood. Mostly residential, its revitalization has edged forward in fits and starts but a renewed momentum has sprung up in recent years. Throngs of people flock to the BAC for weddings, concerts, and public events nearly every weekend. The main drag, North Fourth Street, is lined with historic bungalows, modern condos, and office buildings. For cocktails and craft beer, Bottega Art & Wine, Goat and Compass, Palate Bottle Shop & Garden, Flytrap Brewing, and Edward Teach Brewery all have comfy spaces for kicking back. Brooklyn Cafe will satisfy coffee cravings and Angus Grill, the Kitchen Sink, and three10 have it covered for lunch or dinner.

brooklynartsnc.com

TIP

Consider the BAC a go-to spot for local and regional art. The Summertime Market, Holiday Flea, and Made in NC are three must-visit big events.

36

ALL HAIL THE HOOKAH
AT BARZARRE

Calling all weirdos, eccentrics, bohemians, outliers. Come find your people! The Barzarre, formerly Juggling Gypsy, is for anyone who doesn't fit the usual mold and frankly, doesn't care to. Their entertainment lineup takes on a bolder approach. Think EDM DJs, belly dancing, and circus acts. A contortionist, knife thrower, or tarot reader may be seated beside you at the next table. Bring your unusual talent, your poetry, your best attempt at fire sticks—everything's fair game. The patio out back has comfy seating and it's primed for outlandish antics. Beer, wine, and food are available but their claim to fame is the Hookah Bar. Choose from over 100 different flavors including tobacco-free options. Puff on blends like Rad Ninja, Kiss Kiss Bang, or Circus Madness and let your freak flag fly.

1610 Castle St., 910-763-2223
barzarre.com

WATCH FOR HIGH-FLIERS
AT THE CAPE FEAR KITE FESTIVAL

Forget what you know about kites. The high-flying crafts you'll find at the Cape Fear Kite Festival aren't the ordinary, run-of-the-mill ones that you made as a kid. For three days in November, the skies over Kure Beach are dancing with every conceivable style, color, and shape. When the sun goes down, the show cranks up with Kites at Night, a spectacular, acrobatic light show. By the time you finish this festival, you'll know your way around these compelling "toys" and be able to spot the differences between boxes, bows, or deltas. If you can pull yourself away long enough, there are food trucks, musical stages, and plenty of activities to enjoy back at ground level. It's fun for all ages and best of all, free.

facebook.com/capefearkitefestival

TUNE IN
TO *REGGAE REDEMPTION*

Let's hear it for local radio. Every Sunday, listeners can set the dial to Modern Rock 98.7 FM to hear the "Night Nurse" DJ Kimberly McLaughlin-Smith. She's been hosting *Reggae Redemption* since the '90s, and her familiar voice is just as much music to our ears as the songs she plays. Once that intro hits ("I'm Not Tired" by Majek Fashek) you know the next two hours will be great. For other equally engaging shows, turn to the following stations: Penguin Radio (98.3) gives airtime to new acts but keeps the icons close at hand and WHQR Public Media (91.3) delivers regional news and entertainment through programs like *CoastLine*, *Around Town with Rhonda Bellamy*, and the *Magnolia Fatback Folk Hour with John Fonvielle*.

modernrock987.com
983thepenguin.com
whqr.org

39

SPLASH AND SWIM
AT JUNGLE RAPIDS FAMILY FUN PARK

Once the kids get wind of this place, you'll never hear the end of it. But, when summer is at its peak, Jungle Rapids Family Fun Park is a perfect reprieve from the heat and endless amusement for the little ones. The waterslides, lazy river, and wave pool are only open from May through August, but "dry activities" like go-karts, mini golf, laser tag, rock wall, and arcade can be enjoyed all year long. Cabanas are available for rent and season passes offer a sizable discount if you think you may be a repeat customer. You don't have to leave the premises for food, either. The Big Splash Cafe serves kid-friendly pizza and the like, making Jungle Rapids popular for everyday occasions, birthday parties, and private events, too.

5320 Oleander Dr., 910-791-0666
junglerapids.com

MARVEL AT MODEL TRAINS

AT THE WILMINGTON RAILROAD MUSEUM

The Wilmington Railroad Museum is dedicated to all things choo-choo and housed in a former freight warehouse of the Atlantic Coast Line Railroad. The company, founded in 1898, was based out of Wilmington. It operated more than 5,000 miles of track throughout the Southeast until it merged with Seaboard Air Line Railroad in the 1960s. Out front, visitors can pose beside and climb on a real caboose and locomotive. Inside, meticulous (and interactive) model train exhibits, as well as photographs, equipment, memorabilia, and videos, are on display. The Children's Hall is especially designed for hands-on play and learning and holds a story hour on the first and third Mondays of the month. The event is free for members and $5 for nonmembers.

505 Nutt St., 910-763-2634
wrrm.org

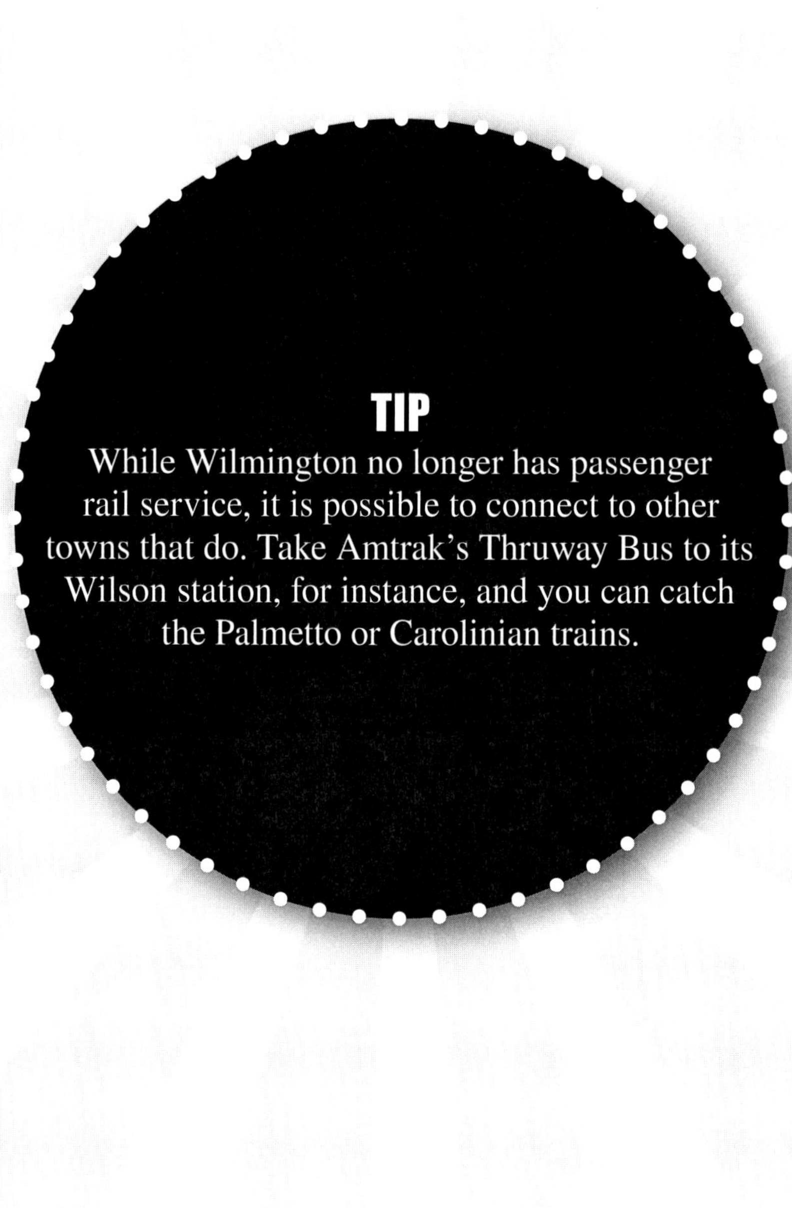

TIP

While Wilmington no longer has passenger rail service, it is possible to connect to other towns that do. Take Amtrak's Thruway Bus to its Wilson station, for instance, and you can catch the Palmetto or Carolinian trains.

41

LISTEN IN
AT LIVE AT TED'S

Tucked away on a quiet corner, this "live music listening room" is a tiny bungalow full of mismatched chairs and a true appreciation for songs. You won't find pounding bass and dizzying lights here—the sounds stand alone. Ted's is all about a distraction-free space for the musicians (mostly local and regional) and their audience. It's been around since 2010 but was taken over in 2019 by local recording company Hourglass Studios. Shows are held Fridays, Saturdays, and Sundays, so check out their website for tickets to upcoming events. While you're there, chill on the outdoor deck and take in the view of the Cape Fear Memorial Bridge in the distance.

2 Castle St., 910-769-6858
liveatteds.com

WIN AT "PENGO" AT MELLOW MUSHROOM

You've heard of bingo, maybe even shouted it a few times if you were lucky, but what about Pengo? Every Monday, the Mellow Mushroom on Oleander Drive hosts this free pub trivia event. It's a perfect excuse to visit the groovy pizza joint, be social, and, hopefully, win big. Put on by the Penguin radio station (understand the Pengo part now?), players grab a stack of cards and vie for the chance to win concert tickets. For this musical spin-off, band names are shouted out instead of the traditional number-letter combos. For the last decade or so, a steady crowd has kept the tradition going, so expect a bit of a wait, especially in summer. Even if you don't leave with a prize, you'll have a delicious pie to show for it.

mellowmushroom.com
983thepenguin.com

Courtesy of New Hanover County

SPORTS AND RECREATION

43

SUPPORT THE SHARKS
AT LEGION STADIUM

Come root, root, root for the home team. A baseball game at Legion Stadium is an evening of wholesome, old-fashioned summertime fun. Along with 12 other teams from across North and South Carolina, Georgia, and Virginia, the Wilmington Sharks are part of the Coastal Plain League. The CPL began in the 1930s and has evolved over the years into the wood-bat collegiate circuit it is today. Players come from schools across the United States and a typical season sees about 48 games in total. A big part of the Sharks' brand is being a positive force in the community so certain events and programs are aimed at families, veterans, and the underprivileged. A general-admission ticket for a home game will run about $9 with options for full-season or holiday packages.

wilmingtonsharks.com

SPLASH INTO THE NEW YEAR
WITH A POLAR PLUNGE

The dead of winter isn't typically the time to put on a swimsuit and go for an icy swim, but many do it for a good cause every January 1. In fact, more than 700 people took part in this event in 2022. Almost a decade in the running, this annual tradition takes place on New Year's Day at Wrightsville Beach. It's hosted by the Cape Fear chapter of Communities in Schools, a nonprofit that promotes strong social networks for school-aged children. There is a fee to register, but your donation earns you a commemorative T-shirt (and bragging rights for the rest of the year). Whatever the reason or resolution, it's undoubtedly a bonding experience and a fun way to say "out with the old and in with the new."

TIP

For seasoned swimmers who want more feel-good competition, the Pier-2-Pier Swim Race, Swim the Loop, and Stoked to Go Out are other annual open-water events.

45

SET AND SPIKE
AT CAPT'N BILL'S

Take one backyard grill, throw in a heap of sand volleyball, and voilà—you've got the perfect family-friendly (yes, dogs, too) setup with a party atmosphere. There's nothing quite like Capt'n Bill's, especially on summer nights when things are in full swing. The lights come on, the music gets turned up, and scads of barefoot players ready themselves to win. While the 10 courts are mostly for league games and tournaments, pickup play is allowed. If you're there as a spectator, the back deck or outdoor bar both offer front-row seats to the action. Try one of the Musser's plates to munch on while you cheer on your team. They also brew their own beer over at Bill's Brewing Company so a Mankini or Wave Break may help to cool you down.

4238 Market St., 910-762-0173
seeyouatbills.com

SHOW TEAM SPIRIT
FOR THE SEAHAWKS

Even folks who didn't graduate from UNCW are still awfully proud of its sports teams. The Seahawks spirit is a rich tradition, and its athletic department has brought home numerous titles and championship wins. Whatever you follow—baseball, basketball, soccer, swimming, track and field, tennis—there's a team to support. Trask Coliseum has its own box office, but you can also get tickets by phone or online. Each team's full schedule gets posted well in advance, making it easy to track home and away games. These sporting events are affordable and high-energy and bring together players, students, and fans with a camaraderie like no other. So, sport a little teal, high-five Sammy C. Hawk on the way in, and cheer on Wilmington's own.

uncwsports.com

BIKE

THE GARY SHELL CROSS-CITY TRAIL

This 15-mile trail is one of the best things to have happened to Wilmington. There are still more sections yet to come but its current layout is a safe and easy way to get from point A to point B with a lot of cool stuff in between. It's also a segment of the much larger 3,000-mile East Coast Greenway that extends from Maine to Florida. Hop on anywhere you like, but for an official end-to-end ride, start at James E.L. Wade Park and follow the path until the Heide Trask drawbridge. For scenic detours, cut off to the wooded trails behind UNCW or stop for a picnic at Halyburton Park. Points of interest for shopping, sipping, or snacking include Landfall Center, Mayfaire, or the Pointe at Barclay.

wilmingtonnc.gov

TIP

The River to Sea Bikeway is another popular route and it connects with the Gary Shell. It follows the old trolley line from Market and Water Streets to Johnnie Mercers Fishing Pier.

48

STRETCH YOUR LEGS
AT THE "LOOP"

The 2.5-mile John Nesbitt Loop (aka the Loop) is where active-types go to see and be seen. The weekends, especially, seem to bring out the tanned and toned, and the path can get quite crowded with joggers, baby strollers, dog walkers, and bikes. It's no surprise this route is a major favorite as it takes you through Wrightsville Beach Park, over Banks Channel, and alongside grassy wetland marshes. It continues along past the shops, bars, and beach houses of Causeway Drive, North Lumina, and Salisbury Street. The best way to access the trail is via the parking lot at the Wrightsville Beach Municipal Complex. Get a ticket from the pay station and the first two hours are free.

townofwrightsvillebeach.com

TIP

Keep your eyes open for "Loop through History" signs along the path depicting stories and facts about the area.

49

GET OUTDOORS
AT GREENFIELD LAKE PARK

This "lake" actually began as smaller creeks built by the Green family who owned the land in the 1700s and worked it as a rice plantation. After years as a theme park and swimming hole, the area fell into disrepair. In the 1930s, members of the Rotary Club, concerned citizens, and volunteers worked to turn the overgrown swamp into a beautiful public park. Today, its 250 acres are managed by the city (with help from Cape Fear River Watch) and its waters are a healthy ecosystem of alligators, ducks, birds, and turtles. The park is encircled by a paved, multiuse path and Lake Shore Drive, a designated segment of the Cape Fear Historic Byway. Amenities include tennis courts, a skate park, playground, and paddleboats. It also houses Greenfield Lake Amphitheater and a Rotary Wheel garden, the largest of its kind in the world.

wilmingtonnc.gov

50

PADDLE OUT
TO MASONBORO

Here's how to have a beach (practically) to yourself. Step one: paddle or boat across the Intracoastal Waterway, through a few sounds and inlets, and head for Masonboro Island Reserve. Simply called Masonboro, it's where those in the know come to unwind and have "Locals' Summer." This barrier island is off the beaten path and only accessible by watercraft so it's frequently desolate, even during peak tourist season. Also, as a Dedicated Nature Preserve, no facilities or structures exist, just an eight-mile stretch of unspoiled sand, thick brush, and birds. Overnight camping and campfires are allowed but you'll have to carry in your own supplies and haul away any trash. The closest boat ramps and kayak launches are at Wrightsville Beach or Trails End Park.

51

CAMP ON THE BEACH
AT FREEMAN PARK

This is the only spot where overnight camping is allowed on the beach. And though the issue of vehicle access has been controversial for some, the area continues to be popular for outings and parties. But gone are the days when you could mosey out there to sleep under the stars any time you like as passes are required. It's easy to pick one up from a pay station at the park's entrance, online, or at Town Hall. If you plan to be a regular, it may be worth it to splurge on the annual permit. Bonfires, fishing, and dogs on leashes are allowed but RVs and trailers are not. Freeman can get crowded on the weekends, especially around major holidays, so reservations are highly encouraged.

carolinabeach.org

TIP

Other camping options close by are Carolina Beach State Park, which has primitive, full-hookup, and cabin sites, and, for service members and their families, Blakeslee Air Force Recreation Area in Kure Beach can't be beat.

DROP A LINE
AT JOHNNIE MERCERS FISHING PIER

You've got your best rod, your lucky hat, and an entire afternoon to yourself. Where to go? At Johnnie Mercers there's more than enough room to plunk down fishing tackle on this 1,200-foot concrete behemoth. The thrill and challenge of pier fishing makes for an exciting day, and the waters brim with mackerel, drum, flounder, and more. You will need to buy a pass to fish (the pier holds the fishing permit), and they can be purchased at the gift shop counter or via the website. Daily adult passes start at $2. They have a full-service tackle shop, rentals, and the store restaurant starts cooking at 8 a.m. Reel in a big enough catch and you may get your photo on the wall for bragging rights.

23 E Salisbury St., Wrightsville Beach, 910-256-2743
johnniemercersfishingpier.com

TIP

With a few exceptions, a fishing license is required for both North Carolina residents and out-of-towners alike, age 16 and older. Visit the NC Wildlife Resources Commission website to learn the specifics. No permit is needed on "free fishing day" or July 4 each year.

53

GET TO KNOW
OUR COASTAL CREATURES

The North Carolina Aquarium at Fort Fisher is one of three public aquariums in the state, and we're fortunate to have it. The exhibits make learning about marine life engaging, and there are dozens of interesting ways to get involved: donate your time as a dive volunteer, adopt an animal, or take a behind-the-scenes tour. Among their many partnerships is one with the Karen Beasley Sea Turtle Rescue and Rehabilitation Center in Surf City. A turtle release is a uniquely special and popular event. Crowds of well-wishers gather at the beach to watch loggerheads, ridleys, or leatherbacks return home to the wild. At Wrightsville Beach, visitors to the Fred and Alice Stanback Coastal Education Center get the rare experience of sea creatures up close on Touch Tank Tuesdays.

The North Carolina Aquarium at Fort Fisher
900 Loggerhead Rd., Kure Beach, 910-772-0500
ncaquariums.com/fort-fisher

Karen Beasley Sea Turtle Rescue and Rehabilitation Center
302 Tortuga Ln., Surf City, 910-329-0222
seaturtlehospital.org

Stanback Coastal Education Center
(North Carolina Coastal Federation Southeast Office)
309 W Salisbury St., Wrightsville Beach, 910-509-2838
nccoast.org

FERRY OVER TO SOUTHPORT

FOR THE DAY

The North Carolina Department of Transportation operates a total of 21 ferries in our state. The Fort Fisher–Southport route (which takes about 30 minutes) is a popular day trip from Wilmington and runs seven days a week with frequent crossings. Be sure to check the most current schedule ahead of your visit. Southport is a charming town in any season but most well-known for its Fourth of July festivities. If you've got your sea legs, go for another ride and continue on to Bald Head Island. This ferry leaves from the Deep Point Marina in Southport, but it's a privately owned company so rates and schedule differ. Something to know before you go: BHI doesn't permit passenger cars, but you can rent bikes and golf carts once you get there.

ncdot.gov
cityofsouthport.com
baldheadisland.com

TIP

Any highway-legal vehicle is permitted aboard an NCDOT ferry, so RVs, camper vans, and trailered boats can hitch a ride, too.

TAKE IN A STAR PARTY
WITH THE CAPE FEAR ASTRONOMICAL SOCIETY

For the past 11 years, curious sky-watchers have descended upon Carolina Beach State Park to train their eyes to the cosmos during its annual Star Party. This statewide event is the collaborative effort of several organizations and museums but it's hosted locally by the Cape Fear Museum and Cape Fear Astronomical Society. The Star Party is one of the biggest events for the CFAS, but they also hold other public observing sessions and monthly meetings at UNCW, which the public is invited to sit in on. This event is free and family-friendly and begins around sunset. There are star-related activities to enjoy and telescopes for up-close viewing as you listen to insightful stories about our nighttime world.

capefearastro.org

56

CHEER ON
THE CAPE FEAR ROLLER DERBY TEAM

Wilmington has had a roller derby team since 2005. It began as an all-female league but the Roller Girls went coed in 2022 and rebranded as Cape Fear Roller Derby. They are still, however, part of the Women's Flat Track Derby Association, which has over 400 leagues across six continents. North Carolina has several, with the closest teams hailing from Raleigh and Fayetteville. Follow CFRD on social media for the latest on upcoming scrimmages and bouts at the YMCA Activity Center in Ogden. For newbies to the sport, the action on the floor can appear chaotic and confusing at first. But get a handle on a few of the ground rules (learn a jammer from a blocker) and it's solid entertainment for the whole family.

facebook.com/capefearrollerderby

57

RUN
THE WILMA DASH

Lifestyle magazine *WILMA* has been an incredible resource for the women of Wilmington. It first hit the racks in 2003 with the aim to highlight the lives and work of local female artists, entrepreneurs, educators, and more. The magazine's reach has extended well beyond its readers into networking socials, leadership initiatives, and community events. Among that list is the WILMA Dash, our town's only "all-female 5K." The race has been organized for 15 years and also features a health and wellness festival. It's a reason to tie up your laces; grab your best girlfriends; and walk, run, or roll for a good cause. Even if you're not a runner, you can volunteer, take part virtually, or sign up to be a sponsor or vendor.

wilmamag.com

FIND
YOUR *OM* AWAY FROM HOME

Hot yoga. Goat yoga. Park yoga. Pier yoga. With so many styles and settings at your disposal, you can trust you'll be able to find a rewarding workout wherever you lay your mat. All you have to do is show up with your best downward dog and breathe. The popularity of this ancient practice has boomed in our area in the last decade, along with opportunities for international retreats, pop-up classes, and specialty workshops. In addition to yoga instruction, supplementary classes for meditation, breathwork, and teacher training are often part of a studio's class schedule. The number of reputable businesses (both membership and drop-ins) have reached well into the double digits but terra sol sanctuary, BeUnlimited, and the Wilmington Yoga Center get voted perennial favorites.

terra sol sanctuary
507 Castle St., 910-465-2230
terrasolsanctuary.com

BeUnlimited Yoga
5725 Oleander Dr., B10, 910-399-4882
beunlimitedyoga.com

Wilmington Yoga Center
5329 Oleander Dr., Ste. 200, 910-350-0234
wilmingtonyogacenter.com

59

LOG

SOME BOTTOM TIME

Wreck diving is a big deal in these parts, and some of the best sites in the country lie right off our coast. The *Condor*, *Gill*, *Hyde*, and *Markham* are a few examples of relatively intact vessels worth exploring. Divers can also drop anchor at a "Meg Ledge" (short for "Megalodon") to search for prehistoric shark teeth. If you've got a permit, spearfishing for snapper, hogfish, cobia, lobster, grouper, or mahi could be tacked on to the day's activities. If you're entirely new to the sport, look to the many reputable dive operators for certifications and gear. They can also captain the boat for half- or full-day dives, shallow waters or offshore, and leave from marinas at Carolina Beach or Wrightsville Beach.

TIP

For an epic offshore trip, consider Frying Pan Tower. Once a Coast Guard lighthouse, it's now an ecotourism destination for the adventurous. The structure is 32 miles off the coast and only reachable by boat or helicopter.

60

WALK A WHILE
AT A NATURE PRESERVE

To learn about wildlife in the Southeast, look no further than our nature preserves. The Bluethenthal Wildflower Preserve at UNCW is a "living laboratory" for students, but the public is welcome to walk among its longleaf pines, water oaks, and magnolias. The university also manages Ev-Henwood Nature Preserve in Brunswick County, which totals nearly 200 acres and is popular with bird-watchers, photographers, and hikers. At 63 acres, Abbey Nature Preserve not only protects native species but an important segment of the Gullah Geechee Cultural Heritage Corridor. Marsh birds abound in the wetlands of Pages Creek Park Preserve, and Piney Ridge is home to rare carnivorous plants. The event center at Halyburton Park offers snake and turtle feedings and ongoing nature programs for children.

uncw.edu
poplargrove.org
wilmingtonnc.gov

61

REST AND RELAX
AT RIVERFRONT PARK

In 2021, the city of Wilmington unveiled Riverfront Park to an eagerly awaiting public. Six acres at the northern end of downtown were overhauled to feature a play area, large lawn, restrooms, water fountains, and the Live Oak Bank Pavilion, an open-air stage for concerts and shows. From the get-go, the park has been an incredible asset to the area, especially for downtown residents who live in surrounding apartments and condos. Its location is well-integrated into the Riverwalk as well as nearby shopping, dining, and parking garages. The Wave Transit Port City Trolley route stops at Cowan Street, too, making it easy to get to without a car. The entire space is tranquil and gorgeous and lends itself to an enjoyable visit, day or night.

wilmingtonnc.gov

RIDE THE RIVER

Over the centuries, it's been called the Rio Jordan, the Clarendon, and the Charles River. We know it as the Cape Fear River. It's close to 200 miles long, and its spidery network of waterways and grassy banks have long been utilized for commerce and trade. To truly appreciate its beauty, and undeniable importance, get out on the water and let the river speak for itself. Quite a few companies operate guided tours, and you'll find their boats moored at slips along Water Street. Many accommodate small groups as well as private charters. Take educational scenic tours with an ecological bent or go for a sunset dinner cruise. There's even the option to ditch gas-powered engines altogether and join a canoe or kayak tour of the shallower, out-of-the-way tributaries.

wilmingtonwatertours.net
capefearriverboats.com
capefearadventurecompany.com

TIP

To take in the river another way, grab a stool at Wilmington's only floating bar, Anne Bonny's.

LET FIDO
RUN FREE

Wilmingtonians take their dogs with them everywhere. You'll lose track counting the number of furry faces grinning happily from car windows. It helps that many establishments are not only pet-friendly, but they're welcomed with open arms. To enjoy a pint while your dog makes new friends, head over to Ruff Draft on Wrightsville Avenue, our very first "dog park bar." City parks, specifically Empie, Ogden, and Long Leaf, all have off-leash dog runs and provide waste bags and water. The beaches do allow dogs during certain times of year but specifics differ with each town so confirm before you go. When summer comes to a close, the Legion Stadium pool hosts a "Pooch Plunge," giving free reign to the doggy paddle.

wilmingtonnc.gov
ymcasenc.org
ruffdraftilm.com

64

WIND YOUR WAY
THROUGH THE ARBORETUM

The New Hanover County Arboretum is a seven-acre public garden that serves as many things to the community. It's not only a gorgeous setting for strolling, reading, or picnicking but it's also an NC State Cooperative Extension Center. Agents are on hand to provide helpful expertise, assist with soil tests, or give out information on youth 4-H programs. The grounds, which include a Children's Garden, Japanese Garden, and Ability Garden, are managed and maintained by a host of volunteers, many of whom have years of experience in horticulture. They also operate a Plant Clinic and hotline for questions about your own lawn and garden. The arboretum is free and open to the public year-round. Two big events that draw crowds each year are the Master Gardener Plant Sale and Art in the Arboretum.

6206 Oleander Dr., 910-798-7660
nhcgov.com/161/arboretum-nc-cooperative-extension

65

SIGN UP
FOR A SURF CAMP

You can't talk about Wilmington without talking about water sports. In fact, Wrightsville Beach was once on *National Geographic* magazine's list of "World's 20 Best Surf Towns." If you're already a seasoned pro, you won't need to look far to find the best breaks. For those who need some extra guidance, look to any of the dozens of camps and classes that operate on our beaches. Most of the businesses provide everything you need from transportation to equipment rental, some offering international vacation packages. As an added bonus, you'll not only learn basic technique but you'll come away with a greater appreciation for water safety and environmental conservation. From kids to adults to family groups, even campers with disabilities and special needs, everyone will find fun in the waves.

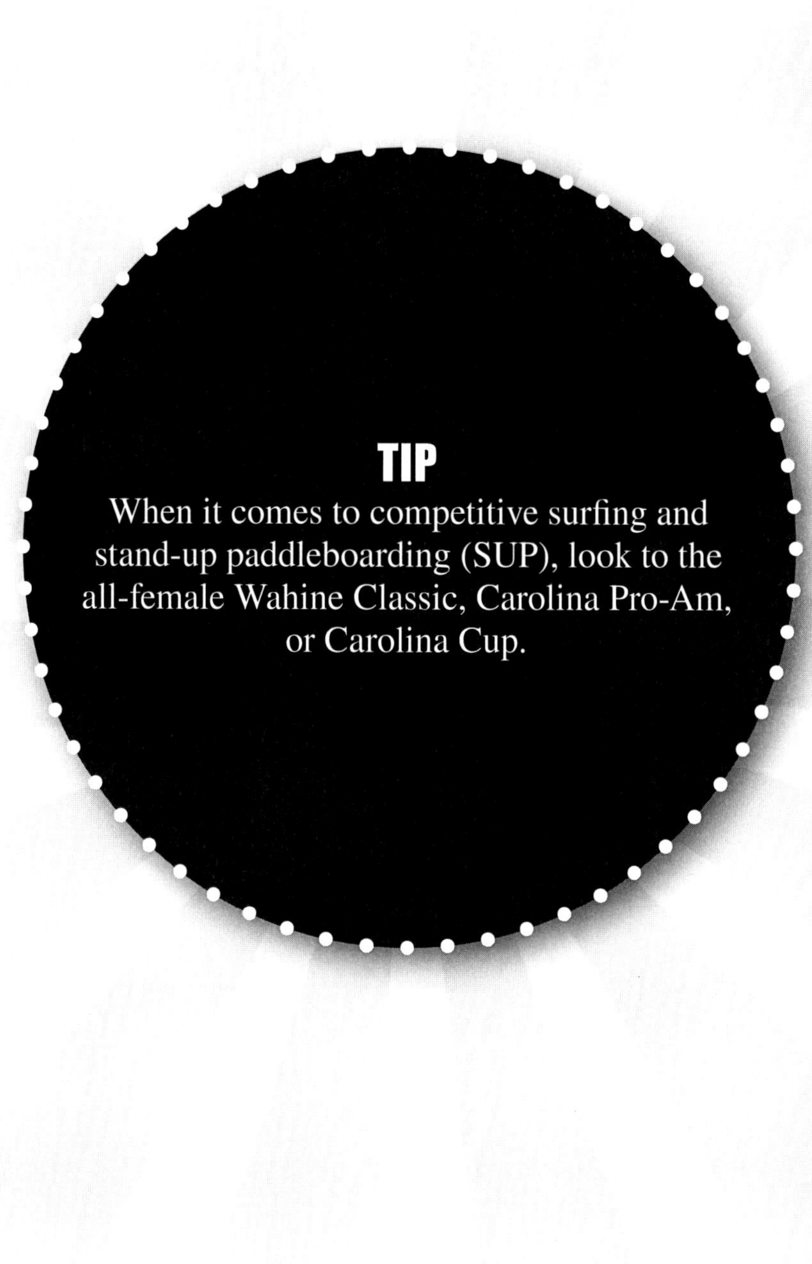

TIP

When it comes to competitive surfing and stand-up paddleboarding (SUP), look to the all-female Wahine Classic, Carolina Pro-Am, or Carolina Cup.

USS *North Carolina*,
courtesy of Battleship North Carolina

CULTURE AND HISTORY

66

STEP ABOARD
THE USS *NORTH CAROLINA*

This World War II–era military craft is our most recognizable and iconic tourist attraction. But come aboard, take a closer look, and you'll see there's so much more to this memorial than meets the eye. It was decommissioned in 1947 but it took nearly two decades before it found its rightful home along the Cape Fear River. In April 1962, it was honored with great fanfare and moored for a final time. The battleship, and adjacent park, are open 365 days a year. Guided and self-guided tours are available daily, but Hidden Battleship and Battleship Alive! are two events sure to make the experience even more memorable. You can also shop the Battle Star Collection, tune into the *Showboat* podcast, or download the Battleship North Carolina app for extra goodies.

1 Battleship Rd., 910-399-9100
battleshipnc.com

TIP

Get there by boat instead and book a Bizzy Bee water taxi from downtown to the battleship's Piedmont Natural Gas Marine Trail Dock.

PAY A VISIT
TO THE CAPE FEAR MUSEUM OF HISTORY AND SCIENCE

The Cape Fear Museum should be at the top of every new resident's list of requisites. It's a useful crash course on all things Wilmington and sure to give fresh insight and newfound appreciation for the place you call home. The exhibits are expansive, covering everything from longleaf pines and blockade runners to African American leaders and 20th-century artists. The permanent collection includes over 52,000 artifacts with photographs, memorabilia, and documents stretching as far back as 1898, including two impressive, large-scale models of the Wilmington waterfront and Fort Fisher. There's an Exploration Station and Space Place for the younger visitors as well as adult nights and fundraising events. Outside you'll find artwork, rain gardens, picnic areas, and free Wi-Fi.

814 Market St., 910-798-4370
capefearmuseum.com

TIP

General admission tickets cost $8. However, the first Sunday of every month is New Hanover County Residents Free Day.

TOUR
HISTORIC HOMES AND MANSIONS

Our city has more than 600 homes and sites on the National Register of Historical Places. Some of the grandest on that list were private residences all within a few blocks of each other. Bellamy Mansion, built in the late 1800s, towers over the corner of Market and Fifth Streets. Built by enslaved workers and free Black craftsmen, the slave quarters and carriage house still stand. The Burgwin-Wright House and its terraced gardens have been a part of the downtown landscape since the 1770s. It has its own podcast, *Burgwin-Wright Presents*, for listeners who want to hear about life in Wilmington during those days. Over on South Third, the Latimer House holds the offices of the Lower Cape Fear Historical Society and extensive archives.

Bellamy Mansion Museum of History & Design Arts
503 Market St., 910-251-3700
bellamymansion.org

Burgwin-Wright House and Gardens
224 Market St., 910-762-0570
burgwinwrighthouse.com

The Latimer House
126 S 3rd St., 910-762-0492
latimerhouse.org

EXPAND YOUR MIND

WITH AN OLLI CLASS

There are over 100 Osher Lifelong Learning Institutes across the country, and North Carolina has four of them: Asheville, NC State, Duke, and Wilmington. The program is geared toward individuals over 50, but any curious mind is welcomed and invited to enroll. Prospective students need only purchase a semester or yearlong membership and then choose from a diverse listing of reasonably priced programs in the course catalog. The classes, a mix of academic lectures and outdoor activities, are noncredit and range from creative writing to wine tasting to pickleball. On occasion, OLLI hosts free special events as well as fully guided international trips led by vetted tour operators and staff. Rather be at the podium? Sign up to teach a class and share your skills.

uncw.edu/seahawk-life/get-involved/community/lifelong-learning

70

STAND IN AWE
OF THE AIRLIE OAK

Oh, the stories this ancient oak could tell. It's been a steadfast fixture since 1545 and a silent witness to a landscape that has changed quite drastically over five centuries. Today, the tree stands as the main centerpiece of Airlie Gardens, surrounded by 60 acres of well-manicured lawns blooming with camellias, azaleas, and magnolias. There's also a small lake; a Bottle Chapel and Tribute Garden dedicated to folk artist and former employee, Minnie Evans; and Mount Lebanon Chapel. As peaceful and quiet as the gardens are, they come alive for celebrations held at certain times throughout the year. Enchanted Airlie, the fall Oyster Roast, and Azalea Festival's Luncheon Garden Party are major sellout events. You'll also find summer concerts, birding tours, jazz performances, and kids' programs.

300 Airlie Rd., 910-798-7700
airliegardens.org

LIVE IT UP
LATIN-STYLE

For 21 years and counting, Festival Latino has brought the music, food, and culture of Central and South America to Wilmington. This multiday event is run by Amigos Internacional, a bilingual "resource, activity, and crisis center." The celebration is held in Ogden Park with plenty of green space and parking for attendees. Enjoy aguas frescas, pupusas, and empanadas made hot and fresh in the food truck and tent area. Face painting, hat races, and a piñata will appeal to the younger generation as well as the many vendors selling toys and huipil dresses. On the stage, live salsa and mariachi music rings out from local and regional performers and the entertainment revs into party mode once the sun goes down and the dancing begins.

amigosinternacional.org

72

UNWIND
WITH A HORSE-DRAWN CARRIAGE RIDE

The historic district and its surrounding neighborhoods are easily walkable, but seeing the sights by horse transports you back in time. As a family-run business, Springbrook Farms has been taking visitors on tours since the ’80s. All of their draft horses are rescue animals, and when they’re not clip-clopping the cobblestone streets, they rest at home on a farm in Leland. Rent a private carriage ride or join fellow travelers in a horse-led trolley. Some of their tours are themed, especially around the holidays, but all of them come with interesting stories and useful trivia you can use at a later time. You’ll find them at the junction of Water and Market Streets. Just look for your guide in the black hat and bow tie. And the horses, of course.

horsedrawntours.com

LEAVE A NOTE
AT THE WRIGHTSVILLE BEACH MAILBOX

At the north end of Wrightsville Beach, an ordinary mailbox holds the heartfelt sentiments of countless Wilmingtonians. It all started back in 2003 when a local couple stuck it in the sand, stocked it with pen and paper, and waited. Eleven years later, it became a time capsule of thoughts and messages—enough to fill the pages of about 130 journals. The original box and contents were relocated to the Wrightsville Beach Museum of History but a second site was erected thanks to a group of UNCW student ambassadors. Anyone who wishes to leave their own mark is invited to do so. To find this special landmark, head to Shell Island Resort and take Public Access 2 out to the beach.

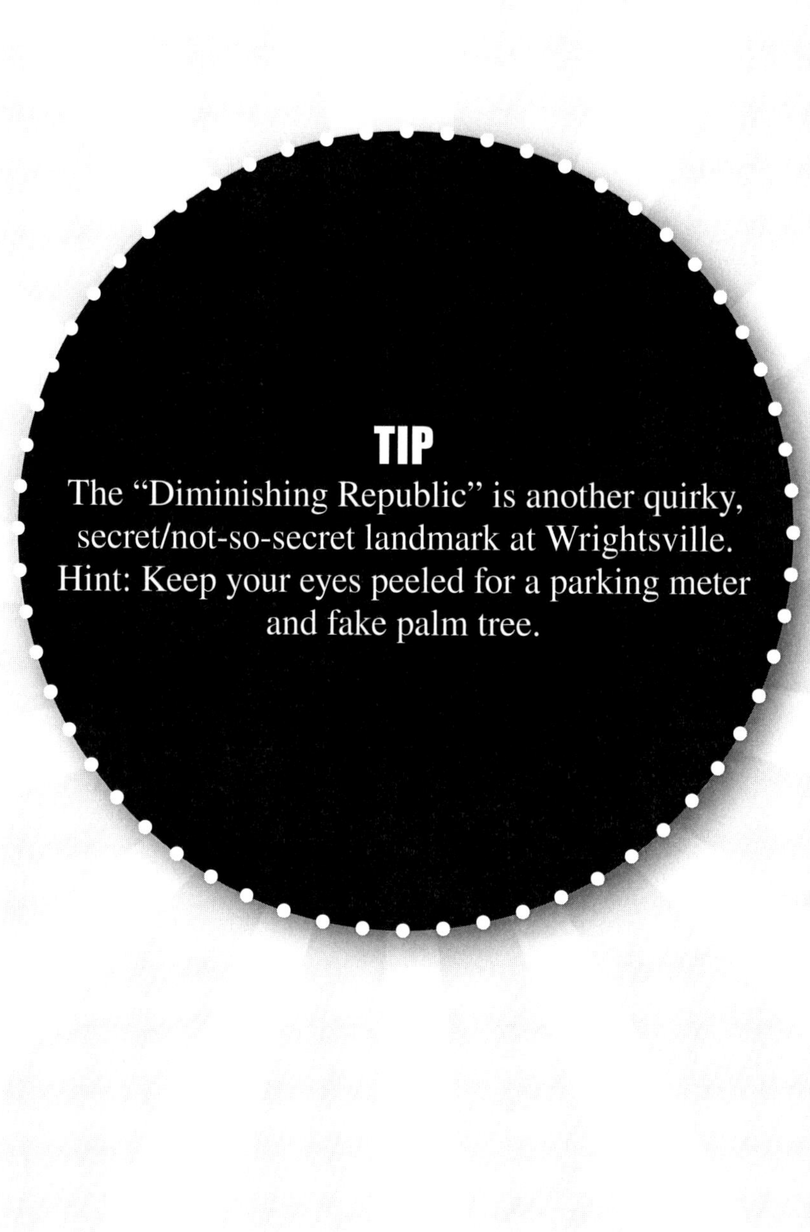

TIP

The "Diminishing Republic" is another quirky, secret/not-so-secret landmark at Wrightsville. Hint: Keep your eyes peeled for a parking meter and fake palm tree.

74

GET TO KNOW

"CAM"

Having just recently celebrated 60 years as Wilmington's premier arts and cultural center, the Cameron Art Museum shows no signs of slowing down. It continues to exhibit the work of emerging and professional artists, both close to home and of international acclaim. One of their most well-received exhibits, *State of the Art/Art of the State*, gives artists from all over North Carolina a chance to see their work on a gallery wall. The CAM keeps a busy schedule with classes, workshops, tours, and programs for children. The art also extends to trails and picnic areas around the property. The cost of a ticket includes access to all of the outdoor exhibits such as the Vollis Simpson whirligigs and the *Boundless* sculptures, an homage to soldiers from the United States Colored Troops (USCT) and Battle of Forks Road.

3201 S 17th St., 910-395-5999
cameronartmuseum.org

TIP
Don't miss weekends at CAM Café. Brunch comes complete with a live jazz accompaniment as you dine.

WATCH A CIVIL WAR REENACTMENT

AT THE FORT FISHER STATE HISTORIC SITE

Fort Fisher was built on Federal Point in 1861 to serve as a vital stronghold for the Confederates. As history would have it, it fell into the hands of the Union Army four years later. Visitors can walk among what's left of its earthen fortifications and will soon be able to enjoy a newly remodeled and expanded visitor center. As a state historic site, it hosts living history programs that are open to the public. They offer a fascinating glimpse into the past using reenactors and demonstrations. Every five years, a full-scale battle reenactment with artillery firing and uniformed soldiers (both sides) is put on. The next event of this kind will be held in January 2025 to commemorate the 160th anniversary of the Second Battle of Fort Fisher.

1610 Fort Fisher Blvd. S, Kure Beach, 910-251-7340
facebook.com/fortfishershs

TIP

Don’t leave the area without seeing Fort Fisher State Recreation Area. It includes the Basin Trail and overlook, a World War II bunker, and a 17-mile beach strand that connects to Bald Head Island.

LOVE YOUR MOTHER
AT WILMINGTON'S EARTH DAY FESTIVAL

Nonprofit Wilmington Earth Day Alliance has been encouraging citizens to take care of our precious planet for over 30 years. Each April 22, it joins forces with several sponsors, vendors, and small businesses to give us a whole day to focus on conservation. Festivities are held at Long Leaf Park, an ideal setting given the pine trees, flowering bushes, and acres of greenery. There's something for everyone: come to get educated on environmental groups at work in our area, sign up for volunteer opportunities, buy eco-friendly products, or just soak in the beauty around you. Like any festival, you'll have more than enough options for food and drink. Put your best foot forward and come on foot, on bike, or in one of the free shuttles provided.

facebook.com/wilmingtonearthdayalliance

VISIT THE WRIGHTSVILLE BEACH MUSEUM OF HISTORY

Most people on their way to Wrightsville Beach want to head straight for the sand and surf. But if you've got the time, it's worth a stop at this small museum, situated in the town's municipal complex. Parking is free, as is admission, but they do welcome donations. Housed in the charming Meyers Cottage (circa 1919), its rooms lay out scenes from life on the island through photographs, memorabilia, and a model replica of the old beach trolley line. Volunteer docents are happy to recount facts and figures or discuss hurricanes, Lumina Pavilion parties, and swimsuit trends through the years. There's even a small gift shop for last-minute beach mementos. On your way out, pop over to the Bordeaux Cottage annex next door for more on beach life.

303 W Salisbury St., Wrightsville Beach, 910-256-2569
wbmuseumofhistory.com

78

STROLL THE RIVERWALK

If the Cape Fear River is the face of downtown, then its Riverwalk is the crowning glory. The waterfront pulses with activity and energy, and the ongoing additions to this wooden boardwalk over three decades not only enhanced it but created a domino effect of other revitalization projects, too. Sunrise or sunset, it's worthy of a stroll anytime and one of the best ways to get a feel for the city. Tourists come for the views, locals hit up the bars and restaurants, and youngsters liven up the public spaces. A few highlights of note are Wyland's *Coastal Dolphins* and our Pedestrian Art Walk sculptures, but be sure to detour for Bijou Park and the *I Believe in Wilmington* mural. Include a stop to the Wilmington and Beaches Convention and Visitors Bureau for maps and information.

wilmingtonandbeaches.com

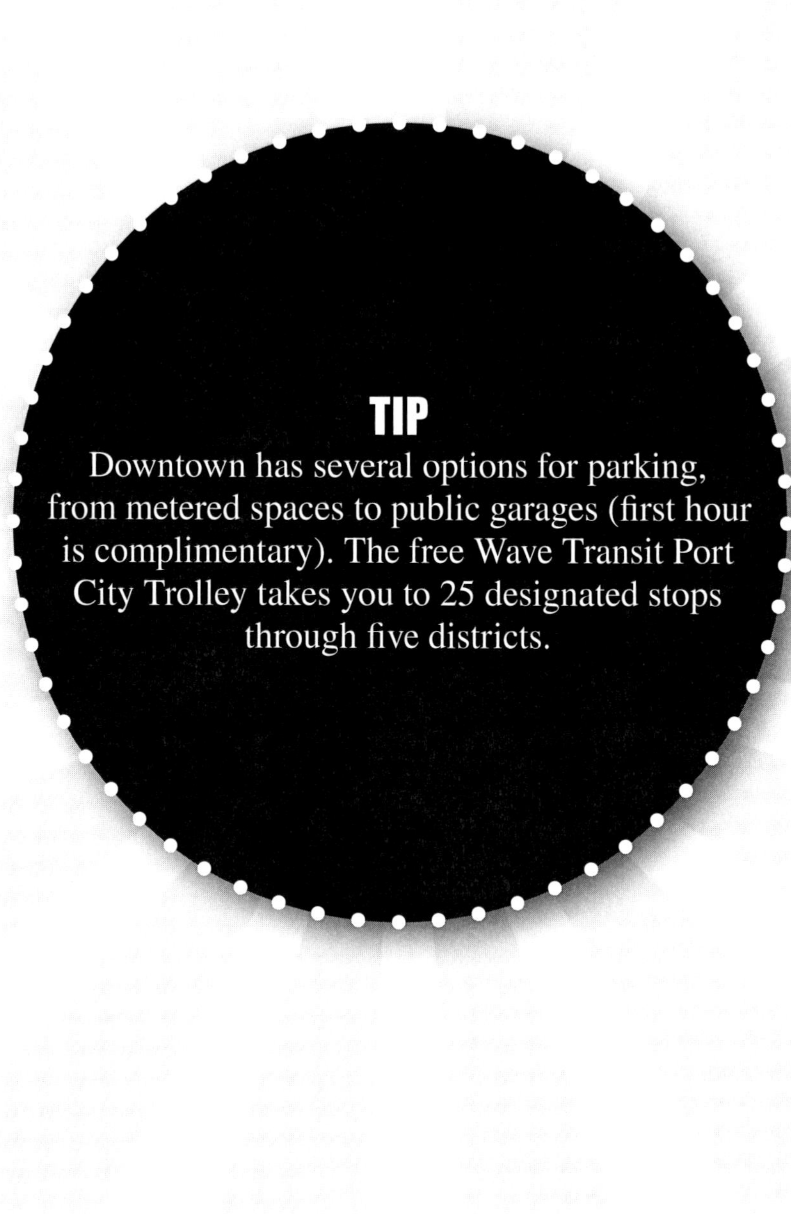

TIP

Downtown has several options for parking, from metered spaces to public garages (first hour is complimentary). The free Wave Transit Port City Trolley takes you to 25 designated stops through five districts.

SALUTE OUR MILITARY HISTORY AT THE HANNAH BLOCK HISTORIC USO/COMMUNITY ARTS CENTER

In 2020, the National Park Service recognized Wilmington as a World War II Heritage City. America's very first, in fact. It earned this honor for contributions made during the 1940s and '50s, primarily in shipbuilding. This former USO took care of thousands of service members and their families during those wartime years through recreational activities, entertainment, and resources. Today, as a repurposed arts center, people gather at Hannah Block for classes, theater productions, and shows, but the building's military past has been kept alive. Guests can access a short documentary as well as a guided tour of their memorabilia via the website. Important federal holidays such as Veterans Day and Fourth of July are cause for big celebrations with social programs, music, and dancing for the public.

120 S 2nd St.
wilmingtoncommunityarts.org

TOUR "WILMYWOOD" LOCATIONS

Here's a bit of pop culture trivia: What do *One Tree Hill*, *Dawson's Creek*, *Blue Velvet*, and *Iron Man 3* have in common? They were filmed here! Wilmington's portfolio of TV shows and movies is fairly illustrious, ever since Stephen King's *Firestarter* kicked it off in the '90s. And despite ebbs and flows through the decades, our little "Hollywood East" has managed to keep its industry afloat. Cinespace Studios (formerly EUE/Screen Gems Studios) has a helpful website for finding past and present projects and where to watch them. And the Wilmington Regional Film Commission keeps up-to-date news on job openings, current productions, and how to be cast as an extra.

cinespace.com
wilmingtonfilm.com

REFLECT
ON WILMINGTON'S BLACK HISTORY

The city's "Guide to Wilmington's African American Heritage," New Hanover County's Green Book sites, and UNCW's Upperman African American Cultural Center are three good places to begin research. The *Boundless* sculptures at Cameron Art Museum and downtown's 1898 Memorial Park bring the past to life through artistic renderings. To learn the stories behind local churches, cemeteries, schools, and homes, spend some time with the WilmingtoNColor shuttle and Burnett-Eaton Museum Foundation for guided tours and presentations. The Black Arts Alliance, Juneteenth Festival, and North Carolina Black Film Festival feature the talents and achievements of present-day artists and leaders. Wilmington's Chamber of Commerce's African American Business Council acts as a resource to support and spotlight Black-owned businesses and organizations.

wilmingtonnc.gov
nhcgov.com
uncw.edu/upperman
wilmingtoncolor.com
blackartsalliance.org
wilmingtonchamber.org

ADMIRE THE ARCHITECTURE
OF SAINT MARY'S

Designed by Catalonian architect Rafael Guastavino Jr., the Basilica of Saint Mary opened its doors as a Catholic Church in 1911. With a brick facade and dome cupola, this "royal house" stands out as a gorgeous example of Spanish Baroque architecture. Aside from its distinguished designation, another interesting claim to fame for Saint Mary's was a visit from Mother Teresa in 1975. Whatever your religious affiliations, the design and craftsmanship deserve a closer look. Step inside and walk around, making sure not to miss the church's most unique gifts: a coat of arms, tintinnabulum (bell), and umbrelino (little umbrella). These items are presented to a church and its congregation when bestowed the honor of basilica.

412 Ann St., 910-762-5491
saintmarybasilica.org

WALK A MILE WITH THE HISTORIC WILMINGTON FOUNDATION

You may have driven past plenty of Wilmington's historic homes and buildings, but the best way to truly notice the fine details that make them distinct are to set out on foot. Once a month, the Historic Wilmington Foundation leads tours for the public. Many of these events, which are usually based on a theme or particular architectural focus, are free. It's a chance to hear about local history, learn from an expert, and pass on your newfound knowledge. Past tours have included churches, heritage trees, cemeteries, and special neighborhoods of note. They last about an hour, go no more than a mile, and are held on Sundays. The starting point is the HWF offices on Orange Street.

historicwilmington.org

TIP

To rummage through bits and baubles preserved from old homes, visit HWF's Legacy Architectural Salvage store.

SEE VENUS FLYTRAPS
AT THE STANLEY REHDER CARNIVOROUS PLANT GARDEN

Fun fact: the Venus flytrap is only native to this part of North Carolina, meaning it doesn't grow wild anywhere else in the world. These small plants have lobes, or traps, covered in tiny hairs that snap closed at the slightest hint of motion. At the Stanley Rehder Plant Garden (named after a local horticulturist and florist), the iconic flytrap, pitcher plant, and sundew relatives dot the landscape of a pocosin bog called Piney Ridge Nature Preserve. The swampy soil is perfect for the plants, while a wooden boardwalk and carefully placed stepping stones allow visitors to wander freely without disturbing the habitat. The park is free and open 24-7. The garden's entrance and small parking lot is located behind Edwin A. Alderman Elementary School.

3800 Canterbury Rd.
coastallandtrust.org

TIP
The North Carolina Coastal Land Trust hosts an annual "Flytrap Frolic" at the garden. It's a family-friendly event that's free, educational, and open to the public.

85

SHOW UP IN GREEN
FOR THE ST. PATRICK'S DAY FESTIVAL AND PARADE

The Irish, and those who love 'em, won't want to miss this different kind of March Madness. Grab something green and head downtown with plenty of time because the St. Patty's Day parade is a pretty big deal for our town, and the streets get packed quickly. The floats start at the north end of Front Street and make their way south, so stake out your spot anywhere in that general area. The rest of the festival continues with plenty of activities for the whole family, and many bars and restaurants share in the celebration with holiday-themed specials. A lot of folks will tell you the real fun happens after the parade once the "hooley" (party) begins and a night of traditional music and dancing ensues.

wilmingtonparade.com

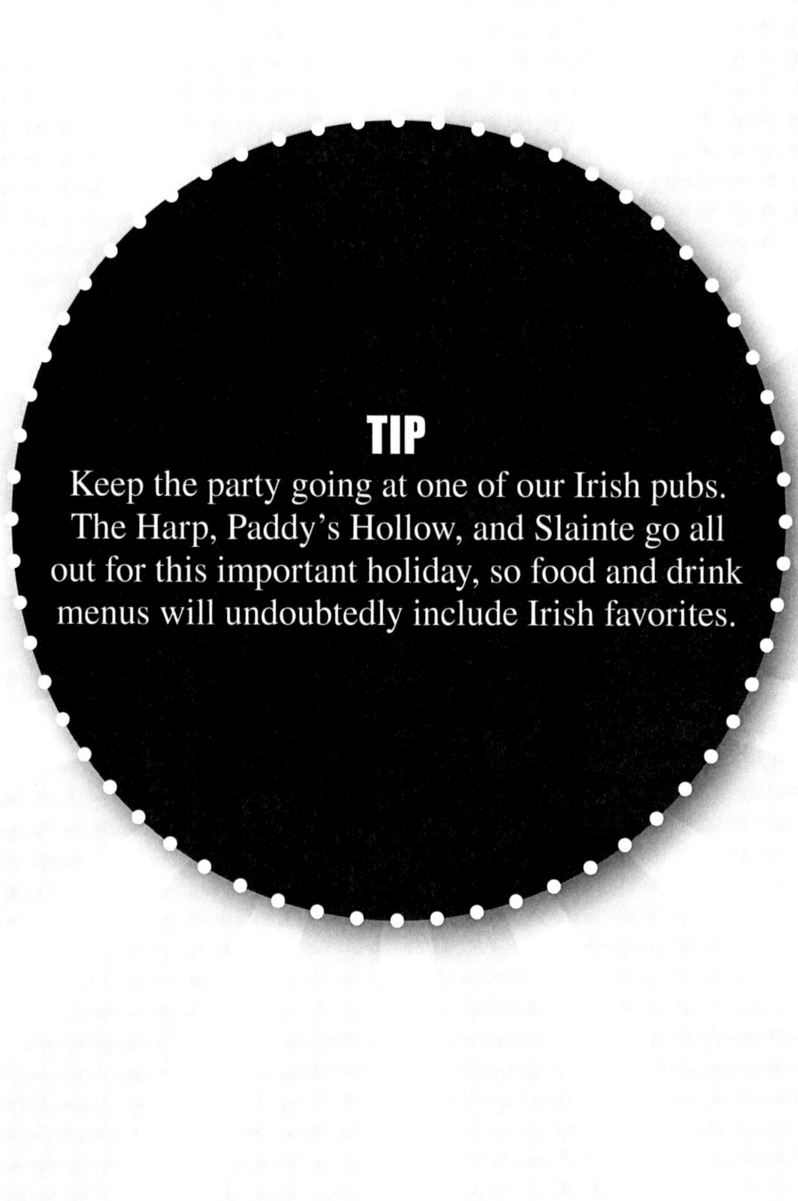

TIP

Keep the party going at one of our Irish pubs. The Harp, Paddy's Hollow, and Slainte go all out for this important holiday, so food and drink menus will undoubtedly include Irish favorites.

PLAY AND LEARN
AT THE CHILDREN'S MUSEUM

Let the kids run wild and have a ball. You'll appreciate all of the learning and they'll have a fun time doing it. The Children's Museum of Wilmington is divided into three buildings and two floors, all with different areas dedicated to art, science, nature, and the like. Exhibits like Bodies in Motion, Discovery Diner, and Wonders of Water are meant to be hands-on, interactive play for even the youngest visitor. Daily programs include story time, arts and crafts, and science experiments, but their website also offers downloadable activities and lesson plans that can be done at home. Birthday parties and field trip packages are available. General admission starts at $10 with discounted prices for military, seniors, and educators.

116 Orange St., 910-254-3534
playwilmington.org

VOTE FOR A BOAT
AT THE NORTH CAROLINA HOLIDAY FLOTILLA

Deck the *boats* with boughs of holly? Yep, that's right. The Holiday Flotilla has been an annual tradition for 40 years. Every November, droves of onlookers congregate to watch this unique parade of lights at Wrightsville Beach. Any kind of watercraft, wind or motor-powered, is allowed to enter the competition. In addition to Best in Show, People's Choice, and the Grand Prize, judges vote on costumes and crew spirit. The route runs through the Intracoastal and Motts and Banks Channels, so get ahead of the crowds to snag a good view and set up camp. Wrightsville Beach Park hosts activities throughout the day and well into the night with a fireworks finale.

ncholidayflotilla.org

HEAR FROM AUTHORS
DURING WRITERS' WEEK

Once a year, UNCW's Department of Creative Writing hosts a weeklong festival dedicated to the written word. It's a fantastic chance for bookworms and bibliophiles to hear from their favorite North Carolina writers, as well as students and faculty from the university's BFA and MFA programs. Other distinguished speakers have included poet laureates and best-selling authors. Many of the events are free, with no registration required, and held at various locations around campus. Some have a virtual option, allowing participants to attend remotely. It's not all readings, either. The schedule is arranged to include opportunities for community involvement. Writing workshops, networking, discussions on technique and craft, and Q&A panels with editors and literary professionals are part of the lineup, too.

uncw.edu

TIP

UNCW's Randall Library is a treasure trove of information and open to the public. Simply purchase a Borrower's Card for $25 (valid for a year) for access to audiobooks, electronic databases, reference materials, and more.

89

MEET ARTISTS IN ACTION
AT ACME ART STUDIOS

At first glance, the exterior of Acme Art Studios gives no hint to the hive of creativity inside. The building was once a warehouse for a carpet business and, aside from the funky car fender affixed above the front door, still looks as such. The original group of friends that started the art collective in the 1980s has come and gone over the years, but a core few have kept the lights on, doors open, and dream alive. It holds around 20 studios and a small, on-site gallery. Most of the artists, who work in everything from textiles to metal to mixed media, only see customers by appointment. Be sure to call ahead or plan your visit during an exhibition show or Fourth Friday open house.

711 N 5th Ave.
facebook.com/acmeartstudios

Courtesy of Mayfaire

SHOPPING AND FASHION

APPRECIATE ARTS AND ANTIQUES ON CASTLE STREET

Castle Street stretches for miles, but the Arts and Antiques District is a compact section of its western end. It only spans a couple of city blocks, but this neighborhood has more than enough cafés and shops to explore to take up most of a day. To sweeten the pot, it's pedestrian-friendly, the on-street parking is free, and it's easily reachable by Port City trolley. Shop antiques at Michael Moore's, bottles of red at Wilmington Wine, or vintage fashion at Second Skin and Jess James + Co. Gravity Records has all the vinyl you could ever want, and Kids Making It sells handcrafted wooden gifts. On select weekends, Curated on Castle Vintage Market and Castle Street Maker's Market set up outdoors at the corner of Castle and Sixth Streets.

THINK OUTSIDE THE BOX
IN THE CARGO DISTRICT

Drive toward 16th and Queen Streets and you'll notice a very different kind of development on the rise. The Cargo District, as it's been dubbed, is one of the hottest projects in town with businesses clamoring to be the next additions to this "shipping container village." The area covers several blocks and comprises an assortment of massive, rectangular boxes repurposed into sleek, urban spaces. In the years since its construction, it's grown to include an apartment complex, hair salon, and tattoo parlor. There are places to eat, as well as a small grocery market, distillery, and coffee shop. Mixed in are offices for coworking and creative media services. Day or night, but especially on the weekends, it's an exciting and innovative community to explore.

cargodistrict.com

GO COASTAL
AT LUMINA STATION

The design of this upscale outdoor mall was inspired by Lumina Pavilion, the famous Wrightsville Beach dance hall of the mid-1900s. There's no fee for parking, and ample outdoor seating means you can take breaks and soak up the peaceful setting in between purchases. Playful sculptures, brick-lined walkways, and well-maintained landscaping add to the shopping experience. To rock your best beach wardrobe, Ziabird, Island Passage, and Beanie + Cecil have you covered, and Oliver and Gentleman's Corner have menswear for every occasion. One of Lumina's most beloved merchants, Airlie Moon, is a given if you're looking to style a room with seaside accent pieces. This home goods store has been in business for 25 years and sells anything and everything "coastal chic" to furnish your abode.

1900 Eastwood Rd.
luminastation.com

93

PICK UP HANDMADE GIFTS AT BLUE MOON

Blue Moon is the place to go when you want a gift, product, or piece of art that's unique to Wilmington. More than 100 small businesses and artists have booths here so you'll have no problem covering every holiday and special occasion on your checklist. Vendors sell everything from jewelry to pottery to food so you can shop for any age, interest, or budget. Not only will you pick up something cool that's sure to have a story behind it, but your dollars go straight to the people who live and work where you do. They'll even gift wrap your purchase so you can leave with a present that will wow any recipient. On occasion, they host special events like demos, tastings, and pop-up sales.

203 Racine Dr., 910-799-5793
bluemoongiftshops.com

WANDER THE STACKS

If anybody's going to see to it that the printed page never dies, it'll be the fine men and women of these local indie booksellers. In an era of e-readers and digital *everything*, they keep on keeping on, loading up shelves with our favorite reads. They play important roles as literary matchmakers, and their shops invite readers and authors alike to gather and share. Speaking of epic stories, Old Books and McAllister's have both been around forever. If only they could bottle and sell that "eau de books" we all know and love. At the little house on Park Avenue that holds Pomegranate Books and Zola Coffee and Tea, you can sip while you browse. Papercut Books carries a wide selection of genres plus games and puzzles for kids.

TIP

Still need more books in your life? The annual New Hanover County library book sale sells hardcovers and paperbacks for a song.

Old Books on Front Street
249 N Front St., 910-762-6657
oldbooksonfrontstreet.com

McAllister and Solomon Books
4402 Wrightsville Ave., 910-350-0189
mcallisterandsolomon.com

Pomegranate Books
4418 Park Ave., 910-452-1107
facebook.com/pomegranatebooks

Papercut Books
200 Market St., 910-660-8607
papercutbooks.com

BUY A KEEPSAKE
FROM THE COTTON EXCHANGE

This historic landmark has a storied past as a laundry, flour mill, saloon, and cotton import business (hence the name), but it almost didn't make it. The buildings were slated for demolition in the 1970s, but thanks to a group of resourceful business owners, it was given a second chance. Just recently it celebrated its 40th birthday. This multilevel shopping complex is a quirky maze of stairs and courtyards, but it adds to the fun of wandering around its shops and restaurants. From stationery to smoothies and shoes to souvenirs, you're bound to find something that catches your eye. The Cotton Exchange has its own lot; be sure to validate your receipt for free parking. Visit the Wilmington Walk of Fame as you leave, our small tribute to local "celebrities."

321 N Front St., 910-343-9896
shopcottonexchange.com

96

FIND YOUR FUNK
AT EDGE OF URGE

Look to this a-little-bit-of-everything shop for indie labels and designers. It's been a huge supporter of local artists, stylists, and brands since it opened in 2002. From irreverent stickers to smudge sticks to bedding and jumpsuits, this store is anything but boring. In addition to clothing collections, accessories, and housewares, they also have a self-care product line called Renew. Check for new arrivals and sale items on their website and socials, or head to their airy downtown store. Having trouble choosing just one thing? Their staff is eager to share their favorite picks and curate a special "mystery box" just for you. And if you have occasion to visit Raleigh, don't miss a visit to their second EoU retail shop on Franklin Street.

18 Market St., 910-762-1662
edgeofurge.com

97

SNAG
SECONDHAND TREASURES

Bargain hunters, take note. There are enough thrift stores and consignment shops within a 20-mile radius to keep you busy for weeks. Clothing, decor, household items, kids' toys—you name it—are ready for the taking if you know where to look and don't mind a little digging. Vintage Values has three locations, and the proceeds from their sales go to providing services for victims of domestic violence. They'll also take your gently used donations, some of which might go to fulfill their shelter's wish list. Ivy Cottage (which is not one but multiple buildings) overflows with furniture, floor rugs, antiques, and bric-a-brac. For clothes, shoes, jewelry, and bags, the Fairy Circle is nicely organized and easy to navigate. Be sure to check their sidewalk sale racks on the way in.

Vintage Values
609 Castle St., 910-762-7720
413 S College Rd., 910-793-4411
5226 S College Rd., 910-350-8918
facebook.com/vintagevalueswilmington

The Ivy Cottage
3030 Market St., 910-815-0907
threecottages.com

The Fairy Circle Consignment Clothing
1045 S College Rd., 910-790-2025
fairycircleconsignment.com

BROWSE SPECIALTY MARKETS

Those massive grocery stores do carry every breakfast cereal under the sun, but maybe it's time to mix things up. Toss out that run-of-the-mill shopping list and throw in a few surprising specialty goods. For meal plan prep that calls for organic or all-natural grocery items, choose Lovey's or Tidal Creek. Both have dine-in cafés, serving beverages and dishes (hot and cold) made fresh on-site. For imported and hard-to-find Asian ingredients, New Saigon International Market is an incredible resource. It's a joy to wander the aisles and survey the impressive assortment of products like chrysanthemum tea, Kashmiri spice, rambutan, and ramen. At Los Portales, the shelves are well-stocked with the flavors of Mexico and beyond, not to mention personal care items, household goods, meat, and fresh produce.

Lovey's Natural Foods and Cafe
1319 Military Cutoff Rd., Ste. H, 910-509-0331
loveysmarket.com

Tidal Creek Co-op
5329 Oleander Dr., 910-799-2667
tidalcreek.coop

New Saigon International Market
831 S Kerr Ave., 910-793-9911
facebook.com/ilmsaigon

Los Portales Supermarket
912 S Kerr Ave., 910-799-7262
losportalessupermarket.com

99

GEAR UP
FOR THE GREAT OUTDOORS

With so many parks, trails, and waterways in our backyard, it's only a matter of gathering the necessary gear and getting out into it. Keep your shopping local and look to the advice and expertise of the people who know our dirt paths and watering holes best. Stores like Great Outdoor Provision Co. and Canady's can outfit any adventure, be it camping, hiking, hunting, or fishing. For all things that float, Hook, Line and Paddle will have you set up for outings of an aquatic sort. Boards galore and Wilmington's "uniform of choice"—swimsuits and Rainbow sandals—can be found at Sweetwater Surf Shop. For excursions by bike, the Two Wheeler Dealer sells new and used models to pedal with training wheels or in the Tour de France.

Great Outdoor Provision Co.
3501 Oleander Dr., 910-343-1648
greatoutdoorprovision.com

Canady's Sport Center
3220 Wrightsville Ave., 910-791-6280
canadyssportcenter.com

Hook, Line and Paddle Kayaks and Paddleboards
435 Eastwood Rd., 910-792-6945
hooklineandpaddle.com

Sweetwater Surf Shop
10 N Lumina Ave., Wrightsville Beach, 910-256-3821
sweetwatersurfshop.com

Two Wheeler Dealer
4408 Wrightsville Ave., 910-799-6444
bikesarefun.com

100

BRING HOME A MASTERPIECE
ON FOURTH FRIDAYS

Every fourth Friday, dozens of businesses open their doors for the Arts Council Gallery Walk. This downtown event runs from 6 p.m. to 9 p.m. and is a perfect excuse for art lovers to mingle with fellow aficionados, sample refreshments, and grow their collection. Free pamphlets, which include a map, are available to help plan the route for the evening, or hop aboard the free Port City trolley to ensure every exhibit gets seen. On North Front Street, New Elements and the MC Erny Gallery at WHQR should definitely be on the list. The Artworks holds down the south end with 7,000 square feet of creative space, and on Princess and Hanover Streets, Art in Bloom and the Wilma Daniels Gallery hold regular receptions with works from the city's best artists.

artswilmington.org

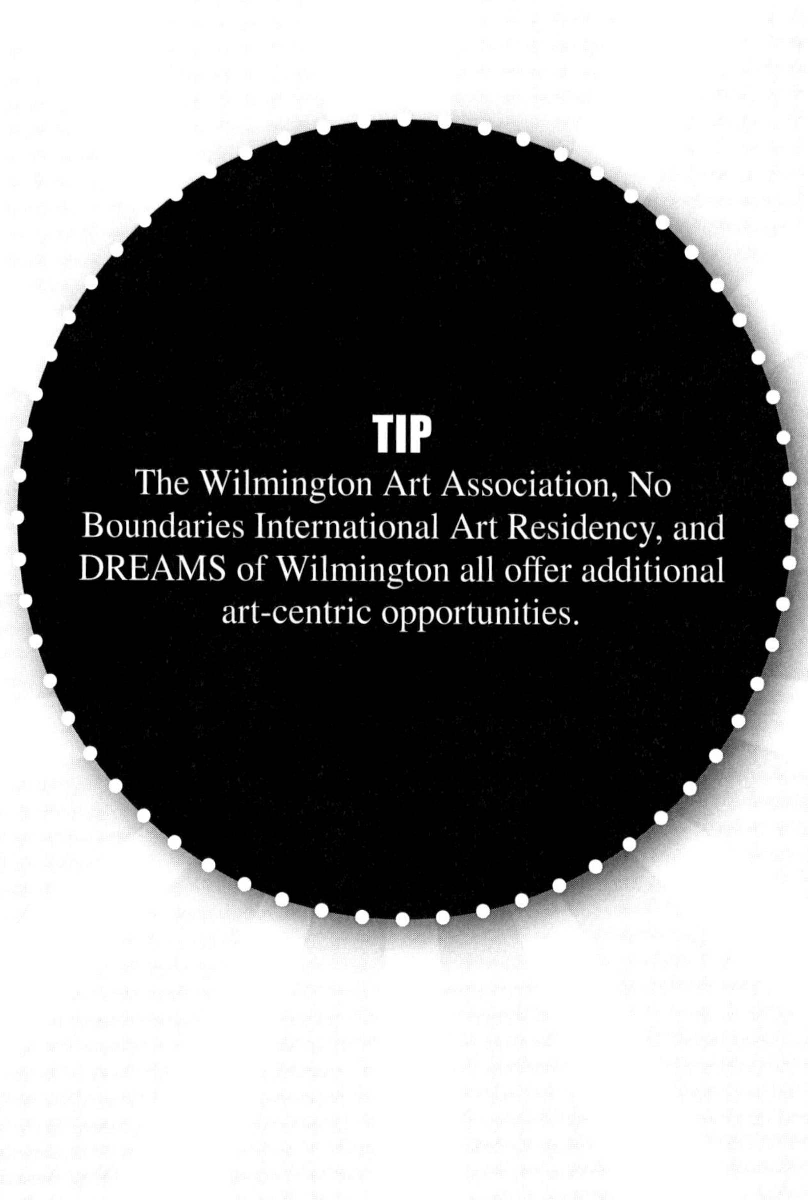

TIP

The Wilmington Art Association, No Boundaries International Art Residency, and DREAMS of Wilmington all offer additional art-centric opportunities.

ACTIVITIES BY SEASON

SPRING

SUMMER

FALL

WINTER

SUGGESTED
ITINERARIES

ROMANTIC WILMINGTON

OUTDOORS-INSPIRED

KID-FRIENDLY

ARTISTS AND CREATIVES

MUSIC LOVERS

FOOD-RELATED

INDEX